Patrick Fitzgerald, Marie McCullagh and Ros Wright

English for

MEDICINE

in Higher Education Studies

Course Book

Series editor: Terry Phillips

esap
English for Specific Academic Purposes

Garnet
EDUCATION

Published by
Garnet Publishing Ltd.
8 Southern Court
South Street
Reading RG1 4QS, UK

www.garneteducation.com

First published 2010.
Reprinted 2011, 2012, 2013, 2014, 2015, 2016, 2017, 2018.

ISBN 978-1-85964-442-3

British Cataloguing-in-Publication Data
A catalogue record for this book is available from
the British Library.

Production

Series editor:	Terry Phillips
Project management:	Vale Dominguez
Editorial:	Jo Caulkett, Simone Davies, Jo Kent, Sarah Whiting
Academic review:	Dr C A Green, Specialty Registrar in Infectious Diseases and General (Internal) Medicine
Design:	Christin Helen Auth
Illustrations:	Doug Nash, Peter Gardiner
Photography:	gettyimages.com, clipart.com, corbis.com, fotosearch.com, Helen Lowe

Audio recorded at Motivation Sound Studios produced by EFS
Television Production Ltd.

The author and publisher would like to thank Google for
permission to reproduce the results listings on page 35.

Printed and bound in Lebanon by International Press:
interpress@int-press.com

Introduction

English for Medicine is designed for students who plan to take a course in the field of medicine entirely or partly in English. The principal aim of *English for Medicine* is to teach students to cope with input texts, i.e., listening and reading, in the discipline. However, students will be expected to produce output texts in speech and writing throughout the course.

The syllabus focuses on key vocabulary for the discipline and on words and phrases commonly used in academic English. It covers key facts and concepts from the discipline, thereby giving students a flying start for when they meet the same points again in their faculty work. It also focuses on the skills that will enable students to get the most out of lectures and written texts. Finally, it presents the skills required to take part in seminars and tutorials and to produce essay assignments.

English for Medicine comprises:

- this student Course Book, including audio transcripts and wordlist
- the Teacher's Book, which provides detailed guidance on each lesson, full answer keys, audio transcripts and extra photocopiable resources
- audio CDs with lecture and seminar excerpts

English for Medicine has 12 units, each of which is based on a different aspect of medicine. Odd-numbered units are based on listening (lecture/seminar extracts). Even-numbered units are based on reading.

Each unit is divided into four lessons:

Lesson 1: vocabulary for the discipline; vocabulary skills such as word-building, use of affixes, use of synonyms for paraphrasing

Lesson 2: reading or listening text and skills development

Lesson 3: reading or listening skills extension. In addition, in later reading units, students are introduced to a writing assignment which is further developed in Lesson 4; in later listening units, students are introduced to a spoken language point (e.g., making an oral presentation at a seminar) which is further developed in Lesson 4

Lesson 4: a parallel listening or reading text to that presented in Lesson 2 which students have to use their new skills (Lesson 3) to decode; in addition, written or spoken work is further practised

The last two pages of each unit, *Vocabulary bank* and *Skills bank*, are a useful summary of the unit content.

Each unit provides between 4 and 6 hours of classroom activity with the possibility of a further 2–4 hours on the suggested extra activities. The course will be suitable, therefore, as the core component of a faculty-specific pre-sessional or foundation course of between 50 and 80 hours.

It is assumed that prior to using this book students will already have completed a general EAP (English for Academic Purposes) course such as *Skills in English* (Garnet Publishing, up to the end at least of Level 3), and will have achieved an IELTS level of at least 5.

For a list of other titles in this series, see www.garneteducation.com/

Book map

Unit	Topics
1 What is medicine? Listening · Speaking	• background to the discipline • areas of study: anatomy · physiology · biochemistry · pathology · pharmacology
2 Achievements in medicine Reading · Writing	• cardiac surgery • eradication of smallpox by vaccination
3 Basic principles in medicine Listening · Speaking	• anatomy • physiology
4 Computers in medicine Reading · Writing	• the use of computers in medicine
5 Causes and effects of disease Listening · Speaking	• defining disease by type • demographics and research methods
6 Biology, biochemistry and pharmacology Reading · Writing	• aspects of biology, biochemistry and pharmacology
7 Clinical setting: acute care Listening · Speaking	• medicine in a hospital setting
8 Clinical setting: primary care Reading · Writing	• medicine in general practice
9 Non-clinical setting: public health Listening · Speaking	• public health medicine • obesity
10 Evidence-based medicine Reading · Writing	• background to EBM • research fundamentals • patient role in EBM • clinical guidelines
11 Current issues in medicine Listening · Speaking	• ethics and patient communication • informed consent
12 The future of medicine Reading · Writing	• global inequality in access to health care • genetic engineering and nano-medicine • cloning • pandemics • clinical trials

Vocabulary focus	Skills focus		Unit
• words from general English with a special meaning in medicine • prefixes and suffixes	Listening	• preparing for a lecture • predicting lecture content from the introduction • understanding lecture organization • choosing an appropriate form of notes • making lecture notes	**1**
	Speaking	• speaking from notes	
• English–English dictionaries: headwords · parts of speech · stress markers · phonemes · countable/uncountable · transitive/intransitive	Reading	• using research questions to focus on relevant information in a text • using topic sentences to get an overview of the text	**2**
	Writing	• writing topic sentences • summarizing a text	
• stress patterns in multi-syllable words • prefixes	Listening	• preparing for a lecture • predicting lecture content • making lecture notes • using different information sources	**3**
	Speaking	• reporting research findings • formulating questions	
• computer jargon • abbreviations and acronyms • discourse and stance markers • verb and noun suffixes	Reading	• identifying topic development within a paragraph • using the Internet effectively • evaluating Internet search results	**4**
	Writing	• reporting research findings	
• word sets: synonyms, antonyms, etc. • the language of trends • common lecture language	Listening	• understanding 'signpost language' in lectures • using symbols and abbreviations in note-taking	**5**
	Speaking	• making effective contributions to a seminar	
• synonyms, replacement subjects, etc. for sentence-level paraphrasing	Reading	• locating key information in complex sentences	**6**
	Writing	• reporting findings from other sources: paraphrasing • writing complex sentences	
• compound nouns • fixed phrases from medicine • fixed phrases from academic English • common lecture language	Listening	• understanding speaker emphasis	**7**
	Speaking	• asking for clarification • responding to queries and requests for clarification	
• synonyms • nouns from verbs • definitions • common 'direction' verbs in essay titles (*discuss, analyze, evaluate*, etc.)	Reading	• understanding dependent clauses with passives	**8**
	Writing	• paraphrasing • expanding notes into complex sentences • recognizing different essay types/structures: descriptive · analytical · comparison/evaluation · argument • writing essay plans • writing essays	
• fixed phrases from medicine • fixed phrases from academic English	Listening	• using the Cornell note-taking system • recognizing digressions in lectures	**9**
	Speaking	• making effective contributions to a seminar • referring to other people's ideas in a seminar	
• 'neutral' and 'marked' words • fixed phrases from medicine • fixed phrases from academic English	Reading	• recognizing the writer's stance and level of confidence or tentativeness • inferring implicit ideas	**10**
	Writing	• writing situation–problem–solution–evaluation essays • using direct quotations • compiling a bibliography/reference list	
• words/phrases used to link ideas (*moreover, as a result,* etc.) • stress patterns in noun phrases and compounds • fixed phrases from academic English	Listening	• recognizing the speaker's stance • writing up notes in full	**11**
	Speaking	• building an argument in a seminar • agreeing/disagreeing	
• verbs used to introduce ideas from other sources (*X contends/suggests/asserts that* …) • linking words/phrases conveying contrast (*whereas*), result (*consequently*), reasons (*due to*), etc. • words for quantities (*a significant minority*)	Reading	• understanding how ideas in a text are linked	**12**
	Writing	• deciding whether to use direct quotation or paraphrase • incorporating quotations • writing research reports • writing effective introductions/conclusions	

1 WHAT IS MEDICINE ?

A Read the e-mail. What do the words in red mean?

Hi Beth

Hope you're having a good time on holiday.

I'm stuck in front of my computer again, trying to finish my history essay. It's 11:30 a.m. and I'm not even dressed yet. Actually, we've got a leak in the bathroom and I'm waiting for the plumber to come and fix the valves, or whatever's wrong with it. He's waiting for a delivery of the parts, apparently. I'm trying to be patient, but every ten seconds I can hear a drip from the bathroom and it's starting to drive me crazy!

Some of the girls invited me to see a play at the theatre last night. It's not my kind of thing normally, but I have to admit the cast were excellent, even if the storyline was not that great. I tried to take a photo of them for you, but my finger was covering the camera lens, so it hasn't come out very well.

Anyway – back to my history essay.

See you next week.
Sophie

B Read these sentences. Complete each sentence with one of the words in red from Exercise A. Change the form if necessary.

1 It's only fairly recently that 'birthing partners' have been allowed to be present in the _____ room.

2 Behind the iris is the soft, elastic _____ that widens or contracts under different lighting conditions.

3 The _____ will need to take the prescription to the pharmacist in order to get his medication.

4 The heart is a muscular pump, dependent on a series of four _____ that enable it to function.

5 Take the patient's _____ by asking him or her about their past and current medical problems.

6 You will be taken down to _____ for your operation once you have been seen by the anaesthetist.

7 The patient was _____ to the Emergency Unit following a near-fatal car accident, and is currently on a _____.

8 The nurse will change the _____ on your wound now, but the _____ on your leg won't come off for another week or so.

C Study the words in box a.

1 What is the connection between all the words?
2 What is the base word in each case?
3 What do we call the extra letters?
4 What is the meaning of each prefix?
5 Can you think of another word for each prefix?

> antiseptic   biochemistry   dissection
> imbalance   incontinent   irregular
> malfunction   microbiology
> outpatient   premature   transmission
> ultrasound   unborn

D Study the words in box b.

1 What is the connection between all the words?

2 What is the base word in each case?

3 What do we call the extra letters?

4 What effect do the extra letters have on the base word?

5 Can you think of another word for each suffix?

b

analysis   cardiologist
epidemic   functioning   harmful
identify   improvement   lucidity
mechanism   medical   palpitation
physician   physiology
practitioner   regulate   resistance
shortness   specialize

E Discuss the pictures below. Use words from this lesson.

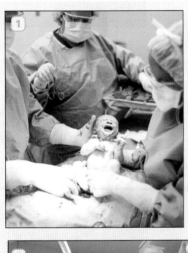

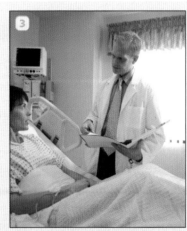

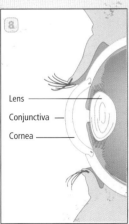

Lens
Conjunctiva
Cornea

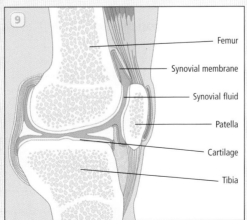

Femur
Synovial membrane
Synovial fluid
Patella
Cartilage
Tibia

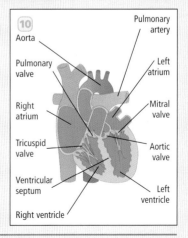

Aorta
Pulmonary valve
Right atrium
Tricuspid valve
Ventricular septum
Right ventricle
Pulmonary artery
Left atrium
Mitral valve
Aortic valve
Left ventricle

A You are a student in the Faculty of Medicine at Hadford University. The title of the first lecture is *What is medicine?*

  1 Write a definition of medicine.

  2 What other ideas will be in this lecture? Make some notes.

  See *Skills bank.*

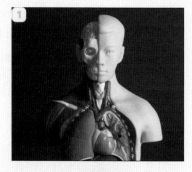

B 🎧 Listen to Part 1 of the talk. What does the lecturer say about medicine? Tick one or more of the following.

  a It is about dissecting bodies.   _____

  b It is about understanding physiology.   _____

  c It is about becoming healers.   _____

  d It is about a lot of studying.   _____

C In Part 2 of the talk, the lecturer outlines the course of study for a medical student.

  1 What core subjects will a medical student study? Use the pictures on the right to help you.

  2 🎧 Listen and check your ideas.

D In Part 3 of the talk, the lecturer mentions *cell* and *scan*.

  1 What do these words mean in general English?

  2 What do they mean in medicine?

  3 🎧 Listen and check your ideas.

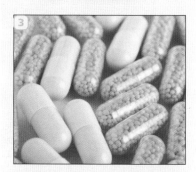

E In Part 4 of the talk, the lecturer provides more detail on what is covered by human anatomy.

  1 Based on what you have heard already, what do you think is the smallest possible unit which could be studied as part of anatomy?

  2 🎧 Listen and check your ideas.

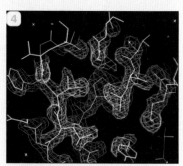

F Write a definition of anatomy.

G Look back at your notes from Exercise A. Did you predict:

  • the main ideas?

  • most of the special vocabulary?

  • the order of information?

1.3 Extending skills   lecture organization • choosing the best form of notes

A In a medical context, what can you …

1 diagnose?   **4** analyze?   **7** prescribe?

2 treat?   **5** practise?   **8** administer?

3 record?   **6** perform?   **9** interpret?

B How can you organize information in a lecture? Match the beginnings and endings.

1 question and	contrast
2 problem and	definition
3 classification and	disadvantages
4 advantages and	effect
5 comparison and	events
6 cause and	supporting information
7 sequence of	process
8 stages of a	solution
9 theories or opinions then	answer

C How can you record information during a lecture? Match the illustrations with the words and phrases in the box.

> tree diagram   flowchart   headings and notes   spidergram   table   timeline   two columns

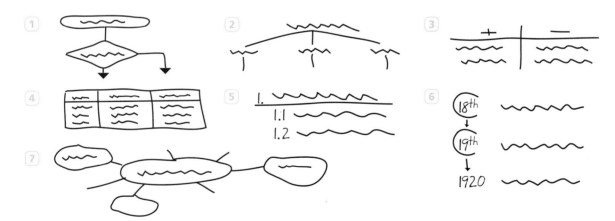

D Match each organization of information in Exercise B with a method of note-taking from Exercise C. You can use one method for different types of organization.

E 🎧 Listen to five lecture introductions. Choose a possible way to take notes from Exercise C in each case.

Example

You hear: *In the lecture today, I'm going to talk about the different stages*

of Alzheimer's and how these can be recognized in the patient …

You choose: *flowchart*

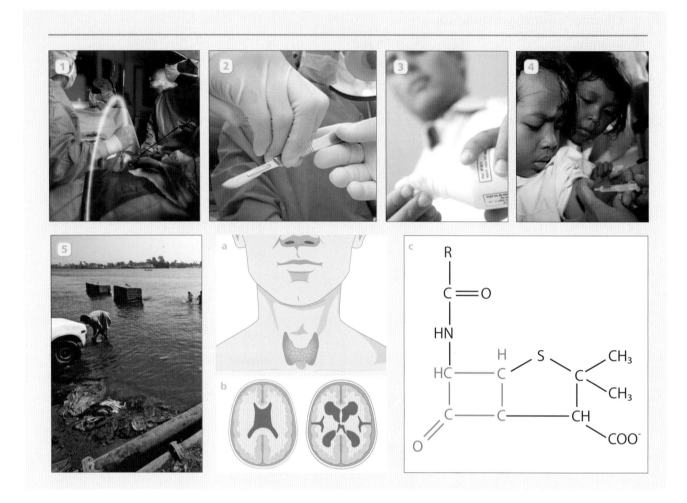

A Study pictures 1–5. What do they show? Use the words from the box.

> antiseptic   laser surgery   scalpel   stagnant water   vaccination

B What does each diagram (a–c) show?

C 🎧 Cover the opposite page. Listen to the lecture introductions from Lesson 1.3 again. Make an outline on a separate sheet of paper for each introduction.

D Look at your outline for each lecture. What do you expect the lecturer to talk about in the lecture? In what order?

E 🎧 Listen to the next part of each lecture. Complete your notes.

F Uncover the opposite page. Check your notes against the model notes. Are yours the same or different?

G Work in pairs.
    1 Use the notes on the opposite page. Reconstruct one lecture.
    2 Give the lecture to another pair.

1

Advantages + disadvantages	Laser	Trad
target tumour more precisely	✓	✗
bleeding, scarring, soreness	↓	↑
length of operation	↓	↑
outpatient possible	✓	✗
subsequent infections	↓	↑
need for extra training	✓	✗
level of safety precautions	↑	↓
cost and size of equipment	↑	↓
additional assistance to maintain equipment	✓	✗
need for repeat operation	✓	✗

2   Key dates in medicine

400 BCE	Greeks – Hippocrates – Hippocratic Oath
120 AD	Romans – Galen – models of body
1628	W. Harvey – circulation of blood
1796	E. Jenner – vaccine for smallpox
1870s	L. Pasteur – vaccine for anthrax
1865	J. Lister – introd. antiseptics
1928	A. Fleming – discovery penicillin

4

3   Stages of Alzheimer's

1. Similar old age – memory loss not noticed by others
2. Decline memory non-recog. new people
   Personality change
   Symp. more evident to others
   low / diag
3. Assistance needed to function
   non-recog. surroundings
   high / diag
4. Wandering off / lost and confused
   2 incontinent
5. catatonic   rigid muscles
   can't sit, swallow, raise head
   Death 8 yrs after diag.

Identify source of cholera

Snow 1854

Problem: Prove water source of cholera
Solution 1:   Microscope + chem. analysis – not successful
Solution 2:   Spot map of victims – potentially successful
Solution 3:   interview residents – successfully identified pump as source

– Note no mechanism identified

5

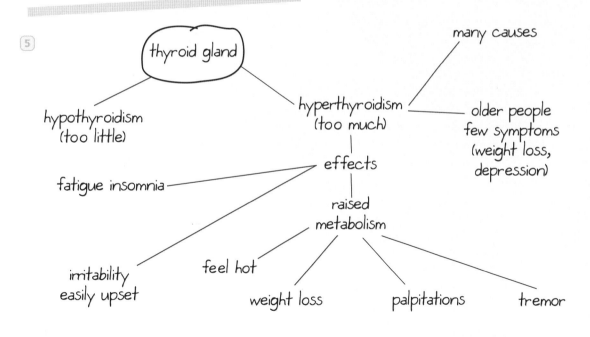

thyroid gland

hypothyroidism (too little)

hyperthyroidism (too much)

many causes

older people few symptoms (weight loss, depression)

fatigue insomnia

effects

raised metabolism

irritability easily upset

feel hot

weight loss

palpitations

tremor

Guessing words in context

Using related words

Sometimes a word in general English has a special meaning in medicine.

Examples:
patient, dressing, theatre

If you recognize a word but don't understand it in context, think:

What is the basic meaning of the word? Does that help me understand the special meaning?

Example:
*Water can **drip** from a tap. A **drip** means a tiny flow of liquid. If a doctor puts a patient on a **drip**, it means that they receive a tiny flow of some type of liquid, usually in the form of a drug, such as an antibiotic.*

Removing prefixes

A **prefix** = letters at the **start of a word**.

A prefix changes the meaning of a word.

Examples:
imbalance – not balanced
misdiagnose – diagnose incorrectly

If you don't recognize a word, think: *Is there a prefix?* Remove it. Do you recognize the word now? What does the prefix mean? Add it to the meaning of the word.

Removing suffixes

A **suffix** = letters at the **end of a word**.

A suffix sometimes changes the **part of speech** of the word.

Examples:
consult ➔ *consultation = verb* ➔ *noun*

biology ➔ *biological = noun* ➔ *adjective*

A suffix sometimes changes the meaning **in a predictable way**.

Examples:
path + ology – the study of disease
path + ologist – specialist in the study of disease
cardi + ology – the study of the heart
cardi + ologist – heart specialist

If you don't recognize a word, think: *Is there a suffix?* Remove it. Do you recognize the word now? What does that suffix mean? Add it to the meaning of the word.

Making the most of lectures

Before a lecture ...

Plan
- Find out the topic of the lecture.
- Research the topic.
- Check the pronunciation of names and key words in English.

Prepare
- Get to the lecture room early.
- Sit where you can see and hear clearly.
- Bring any equipment you may need.
- Write the date, topic and name of the lecturer at the top of a sheet of paper.

During a lecture ...

Predict
- Listen carefully to the introduction. Think: *What kind of lecture is this?*
- Write an outline. Leave space for notes.
- Think of possible answers/solutions/effects, etc., while the lecturer is speaking.

Produce
- Write notes/copy from the board.
- Record sources – books/websites/names.
- At the end, ask the lecturer/other students for missing information.

Making perfect lecture notes

Choose the best way to record information from a lecture.

advantages and disadvantages	➜ two-column table
cause and effect	➜ spidergram
classification and definition	➜ tree diagram/spidergram
comparison and contrast	➜ table
facts and figures	➜ table
sequence of events	➜ timeline
stages of a process	➜ flowchart
question and answer	➜ headings and notes

Speaking from notes

Sometimes you may have to give a short talk in a seminar on research you have done.
- Prepare the listeners with an introduction.
- Match the introduction to the type of information/notes.

2 ACHIEVEMENTS IN MEDICINE

A How can an English–English dictionary help you understand and produce spoken and written English?

B Study the dictionary extract on the opposite page.

1 Why are the two words (top left and top right) important?

2 How many meanings does *medication* have? What about *medicine*?

3 Why does the word *medical* appear twice in **bold**?

4 What do we call a doctor working in the armed forces?

5 Where is the stress on *medicine*? What about *medicinal*?

6 What is the pronunciation of *c* in each bold word in this extract?

7 What is the pronunciation of *a* in each bold word in this extract?

8 What part of speech is *medicated*?

9 Can you say *Your medications are out of date?* Explain your answer.

10 Can we write: *Did the doctor medicate appropriately?* Why (not)?

C Look at the bold words in the dictionary extract on the opposite page.

1 What order are they in?

2 Write the words in the blue box in the same order.

> mass   waste   disc   joint   stool
> loose   labour
> productive   medicated   episode
> carrier   murmur   patient

D Look at the top of this double page from an English–English dictionary.

1 Which word from Exercise C will appear on these pages?

2 Think of words before and after some of the other words in Exercise C.

> **mediation** | **medicine**

E Look up the red words from Exercise C in a dictionary.

1 How many meanings can you find for each word?

2 What kind of noun/verb is each word?

3 Which meaning is most likely in a medical context?

F Look up the green words from Exercise C.

1 Where is the stress in each word?

2 What is the sound of the underlined letter(s) in each word?

3 Which meaning is most likely in a medical context?

G Test each other on the words from Exercise C. Give the dictionary definition of one of the words. Can your partner guess which word you are defining?

H Discuss the pictures on the opposite page using words from this lesson.

mediation   **medicine**

mediation /ˌmiːdiˈeɪʃ(ə)n/ *n* [U] to negotiate or intervene to resolve a problem, medical or political: *This works through the mediation of the central nervous system.*

medic /ˈmedɪk/ *n* [C] 1. a doctor or medical student 2. a person working with the armed forces trained to give medical treatment

medical¹ /ˈmedɪk(ə)l/ *adj* relating to illness or injury and its treatment or prevention: *medical care*

medical² /ˈmedɪk(ə)l/ *n* [U] complete examination of the body by a doctor (also **medical examination**)

medical examiner /ˈmedɪk(ə)l ɪgˈzæmɪnə(r)/ *n* [C] a medical expert responsible for examining a dead body to find out the cause of death

medically /ˈmedɪk(ə)li/ *adv The signed form is proof this person is fit for work, medically speaking.*

medicate /ˈmedɪkeɪt/ *v* [T] to give a patient medication, especially a drug that might affect his/her behaviour (also **self-medicate**)

medicated /ˈmedɪˌkeɪtɪd/ *adj* containing a substance intended to kill bacteria and so prevent or cure infection of the skin or hair: *medicated shampoo*

medication /ˌmedɪˈkeɪʃ(ə)n/ *n* [C/U] form of medicine or drug taken to prevent or treat an illness: *Cold medications are available over the counter. Are you on any medication for your arthritis?*

medicinal /məˈdɪs(ə)nəl/ *adj* useful in the process of healing or treating illnesses: *medicinal herbs, medicinal properties*

medicine /ˈmed(ə)sən/ *n* [U] 1. the study and treatment of illness and injuries: *Radiology is a branch of medicine.* [C/U] 2. a substance that you swallow to cure an illness, usually a liquid

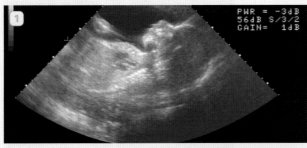

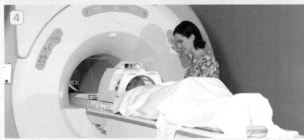

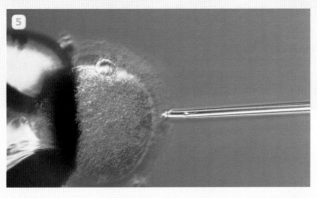

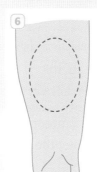

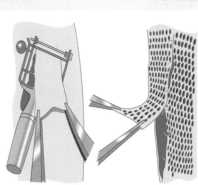

A What are the greatest medical achievements of all time?

B Study the text on the right.
1 Define each achievement.
2 How did it change human life?
3 Which is the greatest achievement?

C You are going to read a text. What should you do before you read a text in detail?

See *Skills bank.*

D This text is about a great achievement from the last 50 years.
1 Think of some research questions before you read.
2 Compare your questions with those in the Hadford University assignment on this page.

E Study these topic sentences from the text and answer the questions below.

Possibly some of the greatest achievements in medical science have been those made in cardiac surgery.

One of the first pioneers in the field of cardiac surgery was Dr Dwight Harken, a US army medic serving during World War II.

Closed-heart surgery was the next stage in the development of cardiac surgery.

However, there was still a critical issue to be resolved if cardiac surgery was to develop any further.

In 1952, open-heart surgery was attempted for the very first time at the University of Minnesota.

But what could be done for patients whose hearts were diseased beyond repair and for whom the only solution was a new heart?

The complex problem of tissue rejection remained an issue throughout the 1970s.

The prognosis for heart transplant patients has greatly improved over the past 20 years.

Such breakthroughs do have their limitations, however.

1 Which achievement is this text about?
2 Where do you expect to find the answer to each question in the Hadford University assignment? Write 1, 2 or 3 next to the topic sentence.
3 What do you expect to find in the other paragraphs?

F Read the text on the opposite page and check your ideas.

See *Skills bank.*

Medical achievements of the past 50 years

- vaccinations
- steroids (e.g., cortisone)
- cardiac surgery
- organ transplants
- magnetic resonance imaging (MRI)
- laser surgery
- discovery of DNA structure
- research into endorphins

Reference: The Cambridge History of Medicine, Roy Porter, ed., 2001

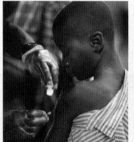

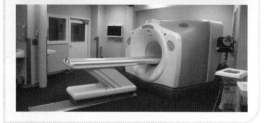

HADFORD *University*
Faculty: Medicine

Assignment
- Do some research into medical achievements of the last 50 years.
- Make notes to answer these questions:
1 What were the initial techniques used in this area?
2 What was the turning point in this area of medical science?
3 How did the solution change human life?

Cardiac surgery: a brief history

Possibly some of the greatest achievements in medical science have been those made in cardiac surgery. The first successful example was carried out in 1896 by Dr Ludwig Rehn (Germany), who repaired a stab wound to the right ventricle. Open-heart surgery itself dates from the 1950s, while bypass operations began in the mid-60s. By the 1980s, two-thirds of those receiving heart transplants survived five years or more. Today, heart surgery is robotized: incisions to the heart have been reduced to a minimum and patient recovery time is down from six months to a few weeks.

One of the first pioneers in the field of cardiac surgery was Dr Dwight Harken, a US army medic serving during World War II. Initially, he operated on animals to improve his skills, moving on to soldiers arriving from the European front with bullets lodged in their hearts. Dislodging them almost always proved fatal, but Harken developed a technique that enabled him to cut into the wall of a still beating heart and successfully remove it. With time, more and more of his patients began to survive, proving it was indeed possible to operate on the human heart.

Closed-heart surgery was the next stage in the development of cardiac surgery. Closed-or 'blind'-heart surgery meant that the heart did not have to be cut open and then closed up again. It was accomplished by passing either a finger or a knife into the mitral valve through an incision in the left atrium in order to remove tissue. Following initial disastrous attempts, Harken's technique was gradually improved upon, and eventually the procedure was made safe. Hospitals across the world began using the technique.

However, there was still a critical issue to be resolved if cardiac surgery was to develop any further. Surgeons had to be able to work on the open heart without the patient bleeding to death. Stopping the circulation temporarily would give doctors just four minutes to carry out their intervention; however, the subsequent deprivation of oxygen to the brain would be critical, resulting in brain damage. Canadian surgeon Bill Bigelow set about finding a solution. Experimenting on dogs, he was able to show that by bringing down the patient's body temperature, the body and the brain continued to function for an extra six minutes on a reduced level of oxygenated blood. This was known as the 'hypothermic approach'.

In 1952, open-heart surgery was attempted for the very first time at the University of Minnesota. The operation, on a five-year-old girl born with a hole in the heart, was carried out by Dr Walton Lillehei and Dr John Lewis. First of all, her body temperature was reduced to 81°F (27.2°C). Secondly, for the ten minutes that followed, Lillehei and Lewis were able to stop the flow of blood, cut open her heart and sew up the hole. Finally, the little girl was immersed in warm water and her body temperature brought back to normal. Her heart functioned properly for the first time.

But what could be done for patients whose hearts were diseased beyond repair and for whom the only solution was a new heart? Successful kidney transplants had been carried out in 1963, so why not the heart? In 1967 in South Africa, Dr Christiaan Barnard made the headlines when he transplanted the heart of a young woman into a middle-aged man. However, despite the use of drugs to suppress the rejection of the heart by the body, the patient subsequently died.

The complex problem of tissue rejection remained an issue throughout the 1970s. It was the discovery made by Dr Norman Shumway (USA) in the fjords of Norway that would revolutionize transplant surgery. Cyclosporine, found in fungus growing in the fjords, would soon be used in hospitals around the world to control organ rejection without cancelling out all resistance to infection.

The prognosis for heart transplant patients has greatly improved over the past 20 years. Survival rates of five years for such patients stands at 71.2% for men and 66.9% for women (2006). By 2007, Tony Huesman had become the world's longest-living heart transplant patient, while Kelly Perkins, another noted recipient, regularly climbs mountains around the world to promote positive awareness of organ donation. Another example, Edward Daunheimer, who received his heart in 1997 at the age of 65 (the upper age limit for heart transplants), has so far lived a healthy life for 12 years with his new heart, defying statistical probabilities by a large margin.

Such breakthroughs do have their limitations, however. Indeed, some two million people each year develop congestive heart failure in the US alone (2001), but with only 2,500 donor hearts becoming available in any one year, thousands are left desperate for an alternative.

A   Study the words in box a. They are all from the text in Lesson 2.2.

    1   Give two common meanings for each word.

    2   Check with your dictionary.

a		
bypass	transplant	
patient	operate	tissue
circulation	flow	organ

B   Study the words in box b. They are all from the text in Lesson 2.2.

    1   What is the base word in each case? What is the part of speech of the base word?

    2   Does the prefix/suffix change the part of speech?

    3   How does the prefix/suffix change the meaning of the base word?

b	
achievement	successful
dislodge	oxygenate
transplant	rejection
resistance	infection

C   Look back at the text from Lesson 2.2. After each topic sentence, how does the writer continue the paragraph? Choose one or more from the following list.

- defining and describing
- restating the topic sentence
- giving more information
- giving (an) example(s)
- giving a list of points
- concluding

D   Write a summary of the text from Lesson 2.2. Paraphrase the topic sentences. Add extra information and examples.

See *Skills bank.*

A   Can you remember all the medical achievements from Lesson 2.2, Exercise B?

B   The lecturer has asked you to research vaccinations.

    1   What do you understand by the term?

    2   Think of good research questions before you read the text on the opposite page.

    3   Look quickly at the text. What is the best way to record information while you are reading?

C   Study the text on the opposite page.

    1   Highlight the topic sentences.

    2   Read each topic sentence. What will you find in the rest of the paragraph?

    3   Which paragraph(s) will probably answer each research question? Read those paragraphs and make notes.

    4   Have you got all the information you need? If not, read other paragraphs.

D   Use the Internet to research one of the medical achievements from the list in Lesson 2.2, Exercise B. Use the research questions from Lesson 2.2.

    1   Make notes.

    2   Write a series of topic sentences which summarize your findings.

    3   Report back to the other students. Read out each topic sentence, then add extra details.

Smallpox vaccinations

One of the greatest achievements of 20th-century medicine was the global eradication of smallpox. The disease is one of the most devastating known to mankind. In 1967, it was estimated by the World Health Organization (WHO) that two million people died of smallpox that year.

Smallpox is caused by the variola virus and is most often transmitted by inhaling the virus. It has an incubation period of between 7 and 17 days, after which symptoms begin to appear. The initial symptoms are flu-like. A significant feature of the disease is the development of blisters on the upper part of the body, which eventually scab over and leave scars when the scabs fall off. Around 30 per cent of those infected with smallpox die, usually within two weeks of symptoms appearing.

The first attempts to control the disease used a technique known as variolation. Dried scab tissue from victims of smallpox was used to deliberately infect young people. Of those infected by variolation, one per cent died, far fewer than the 30 per cent killed by infection in the normal way. Despite the risks, variolation was still used in some remote communities until relatively recently.

However, it was the discovery of vaccination by Edward Jenner in 1796 which marked a major step forward in controlling the disease. Vaccination involves the administration of a preparation that allows the body to develop resistance to a disease without having to be exposed to it. By infecting children with cowpox, a relatively minor disease, Jenner found they developed immunity to smallpox. By 1853, infants in the UK were required by law to be vaccinated against smallpox, though the vaccines used were not always effective.

Further advances were made in the 1920s with the development of dried vaccines in France and the Netherlands. These were more effective but were difficult to store in hot climates. An outbreak of smallpox in New York City in 1947 led to the development of a freeze-drying technique which meant the vaccine could be stored for months without refrigeration, even in tropical climates.

In 1966, the WHO set a ten-year goal for the eradication of smallpox worldwide. Considerable resources were devoted to the development of

mechanisms for reporting and monitoring the disease. Improved technology and better vaccines also helped.

By 1980, the WHO could formally declare smallpox eradicated worldwide. The last naturally occurring case was reported in 1977, in Somalia. The last fatality was in the UK in 1978, following the escape of the virus from a research lab. It was the first time a human infectious disease had been completely eradicated. Smallpox was no longer a killer of humanity.

Smallpox has a number of unique characteristics which made its eradication possible. Its symptoms develop quickly, making those infected aware of the disease at an early stage and reducing the possibility of them unknowingly transmitting the disease to others. Because it is almost completely specific to humans, there is a very low possibility of smallpox being kept alive in animals to reinfect humans. The availability of effective vaccines was also a necessary factor. Finally, the high level of mortality from the disease made it easier to achieve global agreement on its eradication.

Although smallpox has ceased to kill, it remains a potential danger to humanity. Though the possibility of the virus surviving in animals is very low, it is still a possibility. So, too, is the accidental release of material traditionally used for variolation in remote communities. However, the most pressing fear is that stocks of the variola virus set aside for research purposes could some day be used as a biological warfare agent. The proposal, in 2003, to inoculate health care staff in some countries against such a possibility shows that the potential of smallpox to kill remains as strong as ever.

Using your English–English dictionary

This kind of dictionary helps you actually **learn** English.

Using headwords and parts of speech

1 Find the correct **headword**.

These **bold** words in a dictionary are in alphabetical order. Look at the words on the top left and top right of the double page. Find words which come just before and after your word.

2 Find the correct **meaning**.

If there are different meanings of the word, they appear in a numbered list. Look at all the meanings before you choose the correct one in context.

3 Find the correct **part of speech**.

Sometimes the same headword appears more than once, followed by a small number. This means the word has more than one part of speech, e.g., *n* and *v.* Work out the part of speech before you look up a word. Clues:

- Nouns come after articles (*a/an/the*) or adjectives.

- Verbs come after nouns or pronouns.

Learning to pronounce words

The symbols after the headword show you how to pronounce the word. Learn these symbols (the key is usually at the front or the back of the dictionary).

The little line in the symbols shows you how to stress the word.

Example:
/ˈmed(ə)s(ə)n/ but /məˈdɪs(ə)nəl/

Learning to use words correctly in context

Nouns can be **countable** or **uncountable**. This information is important for using articles and verb forms (e.g., *is/are*) correctly. Look for the symbol **[C]** or **[U]**.

Some verbs need an object. They are **transitive**. Some verbs don't need an object. They are **intransitive**. This information is important for making good sentences. Look for the symbol **[T]** or **[I]**.

Some words can be spelt in **British** English (e.g., *colour, centre*) or **American** English (e.g., *color, center*). Choose the correct spelling for the text you are working on.

Doing reading research

Before you start reading ...

- Think of research questions. In other words, ask yourself: *What must I find out from my research?*
- Look at headings, sub-headings, illustrations, etc. Look for patterns or variations in presentation, e.g., a series of dates; words in **bold** or *italic script*. Think: *What information do they give me?*
- Decide how to record information from your reading. Choose one or more methods of note-taking. See Unit 1 *Skills bank*.

While you are reading ...

- Highlight the topic sentences.
- Think: *Which paragraph(s) will probably give me the answer to my research questions?*
- Read these paragraphs first.
- Make notes.

After reading ...

- Think: *Did the text answer all my research questions?*
- If the answer is no, look at other paragraphs to see if the information is there.

Using topic sentences to summarize

The topic sentences of a text normally make a good basis for a summary. Follow this procedure:

- Locate the topic sentences.
- Paraphrase them – in other words, rewrite them in your own words so that the meaning is the same. Do not simply copy them. (This is a form of plagiarism.)
- Add supporting information – once again, in your own words.

Example:

Topic sentence	*Possibly some of the greatest achievements in medical science have been those made in cardiac surgery.*
Paraphrase of topic sentence	*Cardiac surgery is one of the most important achievements in medical science.*
Supporting information and examples (summarized)	*In 1896, Dr Ludwig Rehn carried out heart surgery for the first time, followed by open-heart surgery in the 1950s and bypass operations ten years later.*

- Check your summary. Check that the ideas flow logically. Check spelling and grammar. If your summary is short, it may be just one paragraph. Divide a longer summary into paragraphs.

3 BASIC PRINCIPLES IN MEDICINE

3.1 Vocabulary   stress within words • prefixes

A Discuss these questions.

   1 The body is made up of a number of different systems, each one performing a particular function. Can you identify three systems within the body?

   2 How are physiology and anatomy different?

B Study the pictures on the opposite page.

   1 Sort the words in box a into two groups, according to pictures 1 and 2.

   2 Name the different systems represented in pictures 1–4.

C Look at the words in box a.

   1 Underline the stressed syllable in each word.

   2 Which words have the same stress pattern as *collagen*?

a
artery   breastbone
capillary   collagen   organ
pelvis   platelet   pump
rib   shoulder blade
skeleton   tissue   vein
vertebrae   vessel

D Complete each sentence with a word or words from box a. Change the form if necessary (e.g., change a noun into a verb). Some words can be used more than once.

   1 The _____ are any of the small bones that are connected to form the spine.

   2 Veins, capillaries and _____ are all types of blood vessel.

   3 The immune system consists of _____ and processes protecting the patient from infection.

   4 The heart is a(n) _____ which pumps blood around the body.

   5 Bone _____ is made up of water, collagen and crystallized mineral salts.

   6 The pelvis is part of the _____ system.

E Study the words in box b. Find the prefix and try to work out the meaning in each case.

b			
cardiovascular	gastroscope	intake	renew
cardiopathy	hyperglycaemic	internal	reproductive
cardiologist	hypertension	physical	reshape
gastroenteritis	hyperventilate	physiology	
gastrointestinal	ingest	physiotherapy	

F Complete each sentence with a word from box b. Change the form if necessary.

   1 Diarrhoea and vomiting are classic symptoms of _____.

   2 _____ is the study of the functioning of a healthy body and its organs.

   3 The female _____ organs include the ovaries, the fallopian tubes, the uterus and the vagina.

   4 The symptoms of _____ are anxiety and chronic stress.

   5 _____ is a non-specific term applicable to diseases of the heart.

   6 Until the invention of the microscope, the _____ structure of the body could only be viewed with the naked eye.

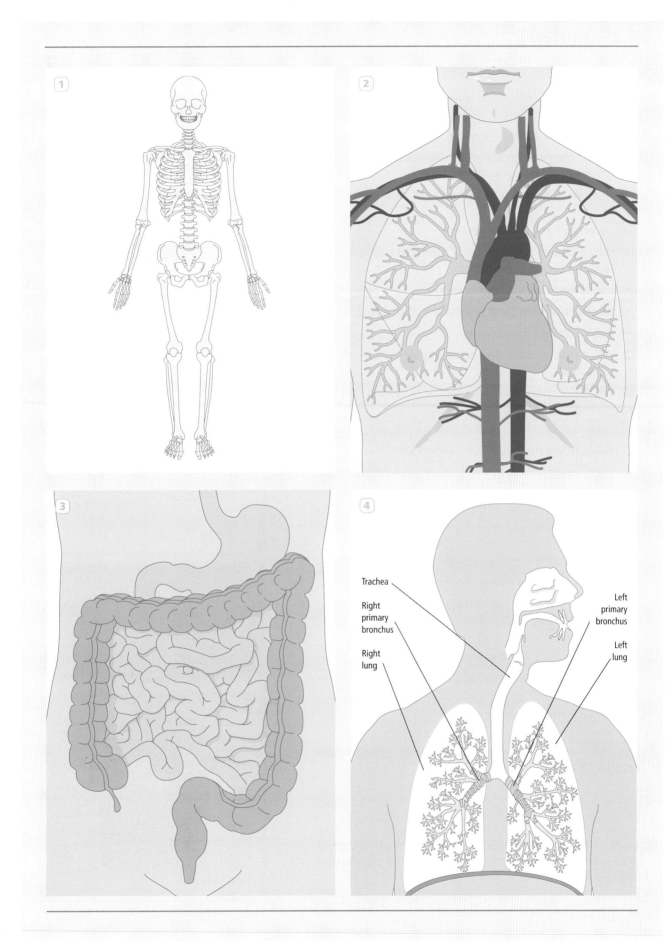

Trachea

Right primary bronchus

Right lung

Left primary bronchus

Left lung

A Study slides 1–4.

1 What do you expect to learn in this lecture? Make a list of points.

2 Write down some key words you expect to hear.

3 Check the pronunciation of the key words with other students or with a dictionary.

4 How are you going to prepare for this lecture?

B 🎧 Listen to Part 1 of the lecture.

1 What exactly is the lecturer going to talk about? Tick the topic(s) you heard.

• the systems of the human body   _____

• the skeletal and cardiovascular systems in detail   _____

• the history of physiology   _____

2 What reason does the lecturer give for talking about this topic?

3 What is a good way to organize notes for this lecture?

C 🎧 Listen to Part 2 of the lecture.

1 What is the main idea of this section?

2 What examples does the lecturer give of short and long bones?

3 What do you expect to hear in the next part of the lecture?

D 🎧 Listen to Part 3 of the lecture.

1 How could you write notes for this part?

2 What are the key words and features of the cardiovascular system?

E 🎧 Listen to Part 4 of the lecture.

1 What other basic medical principle is directly linked to physiology?

2 What is the research task?

F 🎧 Listen and say whether the sentences you hear are true or false. Explain your reasons.

1 _____   **3** _____   **5** _____

2 _____   **4** _____   **6** _____

G Look at slides 1–4 and discuss what you have learnt about the different parts of the aspects of physiology represented.

HADFORD *University*

Faculty: Medicine

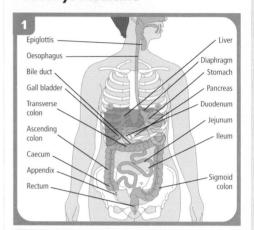

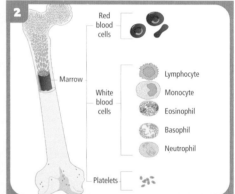

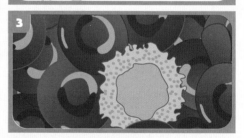

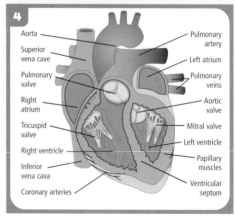

A 🎧 Listen to some stressed syllables. Identify the word below in each case. Number each word.

Example:

You hear: *1 vas* /væs/ You write:

artery ____	hormone ____	renew ____
biochemical ____	mechanical ____	reproductive ____
cardiovascular *1*	nervous ____	respiratory ____
circulation ____	nutrient ____	skeleton ____
digestive ____	organ ____	system ____
internal ____	regulate ____	vessel ____

B Where is the main stress in each multi-syllable word in Exercise A?

    1 Mark the main stress.

    2 Practise saying each word.

C Work in pairs or groups. Define one of the words in Exercise A. The other student(s) must find and say the correct word.

D Look at the slide. Label the different parts of the body.

E Before you attend a lecture, you should do some research.

    1 How could you research the lecture topics on the right?

    2 What information should you record?

    3 How could you record the information?

F You are going to do some research on a particular lecture topic. You must find the following.

    1 a dictionary definition

    2 an encyclopedia explanation

    3 a useful Internet site

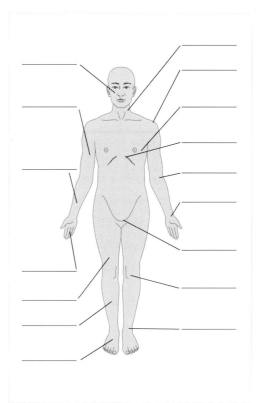

Student A
- Do some research on **terms related to the anatomical positions of the body**.
- Tell your partner about your findings.

Student B
- Do some research on **terms to describe movement of the body**.
- Tell your partner about your findings.

 **HADFORD** *University*

Faculty: Medicine

1 Movements of the body

2 The history of human anatomy

3 Anatomical positions

4 Functioning of the gastrointestinal system

A You are going to listen to a lecture which extends the topic of the lecture in Lesson 3.2.

   1 Make a list of points from the lecture in Lesson 3.2.

   2 What is the lecturer going to talk about today? (Clue: you researched it in Lesson 3.3.)

   3 🎧 Listen to Part 1 of today's lecture and check your ideas.

B Look at the slides for today's lecture on the opposite page.

   1 What is shown in slide 1?

   2 What is shown in slide 2?

   3 What is a good way to make notes from this lecture? Prepare a page in your notebook.

C 🎧 Listen to Part 2 of the lecture. Make notes. If necessary, ask other students for information.
   See *Skills bank*.

D Look at slides 3 and 4 on the opposite page.

   1 What is being shown in slides 3 and 4?

   2 🎧 Listen to Part 3 of the lecture and check your ideas.

E 🎧 Listen to the final part of the lecture. What other purpose do the anatomical planes serve?

F Imagine you had to report this lecture to a student who was absent.

   1 Study the transcript on page 117. Find and underline or highlight key sections of the lecture.

   2 Find and underline key sentences from the lecture.

   3 Make sure you can say the sentences with good pronunciation.

   4 Compare your ideas in groups.

G Match the words and definitions.

1 anterior		includes arms and hands
2 trunk		closer to the median plane
3 pelvis	above another structure, opposite of inferior	
4 forearm	closer to the body surface, opposite of deep	
5 superior	in front of another structure, opposite of posterior	
6 upper limbs		includes the chest, abdomen and pelvis
7 medial		lower part of the arm
8 superficial	lower part of the abdomen located between the hip bones	

H Practise describing the relationship between the different regions of the body.

I Write about the lecture slides using words and phrases from Exercise G.

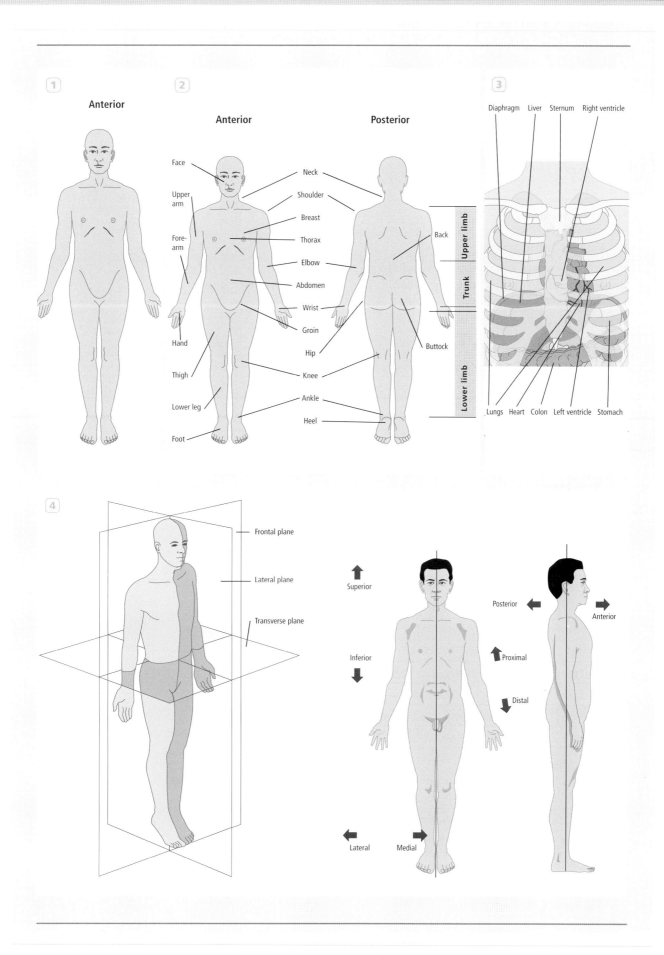

1

Anterior

2

Anterior   Posterior

Face
Upper arm
Fore-arm
Hand
Thigh
Lower leg
Foot

Neck
Shoulder
Breast
Thorax
Elbow
Abdomen
Wrist
Groin
Hip
Knee
Ankle
Heel

Back
Buttock

Upper limb
Trunk
Lower limb

3

Diaphragm   Liver   Sternum   Right ventricle

Lungs   Heart   Colon   Left ventricle   Stomach

4

Frontal plane
Lateral plane
Transverse plane

Superior
Inferior

Posterior
Anterior
Proximal
Distal

Lateral   Medial

Stress within words

Nouns, **verbs**, **adjectives** and **adverbs** are called **content words** because they carry the meaning.

One-syllable words

Some content words have **one syllable** or sound. This is always stressed.

Examples:
'limb, 'vein, 'lung

Two-syllable words

Some content words have **two syllables**. Two-syllable nouns and adjectives are often stressed on the first syllable. Two-syllable verbs are often stressed on the second syllable.

Examples:

Nouns	'organ, 'kidney, 'liver
Adjectives	'toxic, 'healthy, 'lower
Verbs	re'new, di'gest, trans'port

Exceptions:

Nouns	fa'tigue, di'sease
Adjectives	u'nique, e'rect,
Verbs	'damage, 'strengthen

Multi-syllable words

Some content words have **three or more syllables**. Multi-syllable words are often stressed three syllables from the end.

Examples:
Ooo   oOoo   ooOoo

This is true for most words ending in:

~ize~ise~yze	'analyze, 'mechanize
~sis	pa'ralysis, di'alysis, a'nalysis
~ate	'carbonate, 'calculate
~ify	'rectify, 'classify
~phere	'hemisphere
~ical	'physical, 'medical
~ity	immo'bility, mor'tality
~ular	'muscular, cardio'vascular
~ology	physi'ology, cardi'ology
~al	'medial, 'proximal, 'lateral

Exceptions:
Multi-syllable words ending in the following letters are normally stressed two syllables from the end.

~ic	ana'bolic, paedi'atric
~tion	con'dition, nu'trition
~cian	phy'sician
~sion	sus'pension
~ent	de'ficient

Getting information from other people

From the lecturer

We can sometimes ask a lecturer questions at the end of a lecture. Introduce each question in a polite or tentative way.

Examples:
Could you go over the bit about *the skeletal system* ***again***?
I didn't quite understand what you said about *gastrointestinal physiology.*
I wonder if you could repeat *the names of the three types of blood vessel?*
Would you mind giving *the source of that quotation* ***again***?

From other students

It is a good idea to ask other students after a lecture for information to complete your notes.

Examples:
What did the lecturer say about *the immune system?*
Why did he talk about *the heart bypass patient?*
I didn't get the bit about *the heart being a mechanism.*

Be polite!

In some situations, it can sound impolite to ask people a direct question. We often add a polite introduction.

Examples:
Does the heart pump 14,000 or 40,000 litres of blood a day?
　　➔ (polite) ***Do you know if*** *the heart pumps 14,000 or 40,000 litres of blood a day?*
What does 'cardiovascular' mean?
　　➔ (polite) ***Can you remember what*** *'cardiovascular' means?*

Reporting information to other people

We often have to report research findings to a tutor or other students in a seminar. Make sure you can give:
- sources – books, articles, writers, publication dates
- quotes – in the writer's own words
- summary findings – in your own words

4 COMPUTERS IN MEDICINE

A Study the words and phrases in box a.

1 Which words or phrases relate to computers and the Internet? Which relate to books and libraries? Identify the two groups of words.

2 Find pairs of words and phrases with similar meanings, one from each group.

3 Check your ideas with the first part of *The Computer Jargon Buster* on the opposite page.

B Complete the instructions for using the Learning Resource Centre with words or phrases from box a.

C Study the abbreviations and acronyms in box b.

1 How do you say each one?

2 Divide them into two groups:

- abbreviations

- acronyms

See Vocabulary bank.

> **b**
> CAL   DVD   HTML   HTTP
> ISP   LCD   MESH   PACS
> PDF   PIN   ROM   URL   USB
> WAN   WWW

D Test each other on the items in Exercise C.

1 What do the letters stand for in each case?

2 What do they mean?

3 Check your ideas with the second part of *The Computer Jargon Buster* on the opposite page.

E Study the nouns in box c.

1 Make a verb from each noun.

2 Make another noun from the verb.

> **c**
> class   computer
> digit   identity

> **a**
> book   browse/search
> catalogue   close
> cross-reference   database   e-book
> e-journal   exit/log off   hyperlink
> index   journal   library
> log in/log on   look up   menu
> open   page
> search engine results
> table of contents   web page
> World Wide Web

HADFORD *University*

Learning Resource Centre

Instructions for use:

If you want to access web pages on the _____, you must first _____ to the university Intranet with your username and password. You can use any _____, but the default is Google. _____ for web pages by typing one or more keywords in the search box and clicking on **Search** or pressing **Enter**. When the results appear, click on a _____ (highlighted in blue) to go to the web page. Click on **Back** to return to the results listing.

You can also use the university _____ of learning resources. Click on **Medical Resources** on the main _____.

Computer Weekly International magazine

The Computer Jargon Buster

There are many common words used about books and libraries which are translated into jargon words when we talk about using computers and the Internet for similar functions.

books	e-books
journals	e-journals
index	search engine results
cross-reference	hyperlink
catalogue	database
library	World Wide Web
table of contents	menu
look up	browse/search
page	web page
open	log in/log on
close	exit/log off

There are many abbreviations and acronyms in computing. Learn some useful ones.

Abbr./Acr.	What it stands for	What it means
CAL	computer-assisted learning	using computers to help you learn
DVD	digital versatile disk	a disk for storing data, including sound and pictures
HTML	hypertext markup language	a way to write documents so they can be displayed
HTTP	hypertext transfer protocol	a set of rules for transferring files on the WWW, usually included at the beginning of a website address (e.g., http://www. ...)
ISP	Internet service provider	a company that enables access to the Internet
LCD	liquid crystal display	the kind of screen you get on many laptops
MESH	medical subject headings	standard subject headings for searching medical databases
PACS	Picture Archiving and Communication System	a computerized system for taking and storing X-rays, CT-scans, ultrasound scans and other digital images
PDF	portable document format	an electronic document format which prints the same on all printers
PIN	personal identification number	a collection of numbers or letters which are used like a password to identify someone
ROM	read-only memory	a type of permanent computer or disk memory that stores information that can be read or used but not changed
URL	uniform resource locator	a website address, e.g., http://www.garneteducation.com
USB	universal serial bus	a standard way to connect things like printers and scanners to a computer
WAN	wide area network	a way of connecting computers in different places, often very far apart
WWW	World Wide Web	a huge collection of documents that are connected by hypertext links and can be accessed through the Internet

A Discuss these questions.

   1 In what ways can computers be used in medicine? Make a list.

   2 In your opinion, what has been the most important development in the use of computers in medicine?

B Look at the title of the text on the opposite page.

   1 What will the text be about?

   2 How can computers in medicine benefit patients?

   3 Write some questions that you would like the text to answer.

C Work in pairs. Look at pictures 1, 2 and 3.

   1 Choose a picture. Describe it. Can your partner guess which one it is?

   2 What do the pictures show?

D One student wrote some ideas about computers in medicine before reading the text on the opposite page.

   1 Write **A** (I agree), **D** (I disagree) or **?** (I'm not sure) next to the handwritten ideas about computers in medicine in the box below.

   2 Add any other ideas you have.

E Look at the text on the opposite page.

   1 Identify the topic sentences in each of the paragraphs.

   2 What do think each paragraph will be about?

F Read the text and check your predictions.

G Does the writer of the text agree or disagree with the ideas in Exercise D?

H Study the notes a student made in the margin of the text on the opposite page.

   1 What ideas are in the other paragraphs? Write some key words.

   2 Which words introduce new ideas in each paragraph?

   See Skills bank.

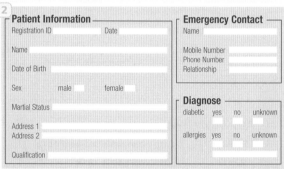

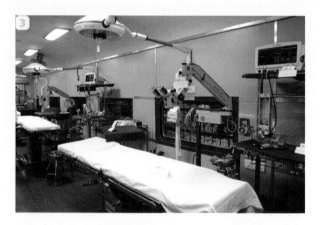

Early computers were well suited to the complex nature of medicine. ___

Computers are good for patient records. ___

Technical barriers currently represent the greatest challenge for medical informatics. ___

Computers are increasingly expensive. ___

Computing from basement to bedside

Limitations

The use of computers in areas related to medicine dates from the mid-1960s. At that time, computers were very large, often stored in basements because of their bulk, and very costly. Their main use – automating simple repetitive tasks – was not well suited to the complex nature of medicine, though they had potential uses in related areas. An example of this was the use of computers to automate the creation of Index Medicus, an index of articles published in medical journals. Subsequently, the database was made available online, under the name Medline, increasing speed and efficiency in locating relevant articles. Computers also began to be used in laboratories in simple testing and for making results available.

Example

However, during the 1970s, as computers became slightly smaller and less expensive, possibilities for their use in patient care began to be explored. A major step forward was the establishment of medical informatics as a discipline in 1977, which considered issues relating to the acquisition, analysis and dissemination of information in the health care process. Because of the relatively low processing power of computers at the time, medical informatics remained largely theoretical. Practical uses for computers in hospitals were largely limited to administration, such as keeping track of bills and sending out invoices.

lower-cost computers

benefits

By the mid-1980s, a new and far more practical approach to medical informatics was becoming possible. The fall in the cost of computing power, a result of the development of the PC by IBM in 1980, meant that theoretical research could now be tested in practice. One consequence of this was an increase in the number of hospitals and medical practices using computers to keep track of patient records. Electronic patient records offered huge advantages over paper records in terms of saving on storage space, very quick access and relatively easy back-ups. In addition, research on illnesses using data from patient records could now be carried out using software to automatically run reports. By the end of the 1980s, most hospitals and practices had at least one computer handling patient records.

The development of the Internet from the early 1990s onwards marked another phase in the use of computers in medicine. As data could now be quickly and cheaply transmitted around the world, it seemed that the potential benefits of telemedicine (medicine at a distance) could now be realized. These included the possibility of doctors monitoring patients remotely, using sensors on their bodies to capture data on vital signs and allowing the diagnosis of various conditions. Telesurgery, a branch of telemedicine, would allow generalist surgeons to receive advice and guidance from specialist surgeons, based on images of their operations transmitted in real time. Operations could also be conducted at a distance, without the physical presence of the surgeon.

Unfortunately, while some of these benefits have been realized, the potential of the Internet in telemedicine has yet to be fully exploited. One area where computing has been fully exploited is in the introduction of PACS (Picture Archiving and Communications System). This is a major technological breakthrough which allows X-ray images to be digitally acquired and stored. It is now seen as the standard technology for X-rays, and new machines conform to this specification. However, despite these technological advances, barriers remain in fully integrating the technology into daily practice. Unresolved legal and ethical issues impose considerable constraints on the exchange of medical records in electronic form between care providers. This means that X-rays, which technologically can be accessed from anywhere in the world, may remain inaccessible to a doctor in a neighboring hospital. Issues such as these clearly present the discipline of medical informatics with an ongoing challenge.

A Discuss these questions.

  1 You want to find out about computers in medicine now. Where would you look for the information? Why?

  2 What keywords would you use to make this search? Why?

B Your search produces 50 results. How can you select the most useful ones without reading all of them? Look at the list of criteria on the right and put a tick or '?'.

C You have some more research tasks (below). Choose up to three keywords or phrases for each search.

  1 Which hospital was the first to use computers for its medical records?

  2 Name one type of operation which has been carried out using telesurgery.

  3 Name a supplier of PACS equipment.

D Go to a computer and try out your chosen keywords.

<u>Criteria for choosing to read a result</u>

It contains all of my keywords. ____

The document comes from a journal. ____

It is in the first ten. ____

It has this year's date. ____

It is a large document. ____

The website address ends in .org ____

The website address ends in .edu ____

The website address contains .ac ____

It is a PDF file. ____

It refers to medicine. ____

It refers to a person I know (of). ____

It refers to an organization I know (of). ____

A What information is contained in the results listings of a search engine?

  1 Make a list.

  2 Check with the results listing on the opposite page.

B Scan the results listing. Answer these questions.

  1 What keywords were entered?

  2 Why was *journal* used as a keyword? Why is it not in inverted commas?

C Answer these questions.

  1 Which results contain abbreviations or acronyms?

  2 Where is each website address?

  3 Which are PDF documents?

  4 Which documents have dates?

  5 Why are the words in different colours?

  6 Which results refer to a journal?

  7 Which results come from educational sites?

  8 Which results come from commercial sites?

  9 What does *similar pages* mean?

  10 What does *cached* mean?

D Continue your research on computers in medicine now by entering the keywords into a search engine and accessing three of the results. Compare your findings with other students.

E Choose the most interesting result. Write a paragraph about the information you discovered. Develop the topic within the paragraph with discourse markers and stance markers.

See Skills bank.

Google

Sign in

"medical informatics" + "latest developments" + journal   (Search)   Advanced Search   Preferences

Web   Results **1 - 9** of about 9 for "medical informatics" "latest developments" journal (0.21 sec)

[1] International Journal of Medical Informatics
IJMI provides an international medium for dissemination of original research and reviews on **latest developments** in the field of **medical informatics**.
linkinghub.elsevier.com/retrieve/ijm/about.htm

[2] [PDF] Japan Journal of Medical Informatics
Official journal of the Japan Association for Medical Informatics.
Refereed papers on latest developments in medical informatics and related …
www.jami.jp/document/doc/english/about_jjmi.pdf 28 May 2008 - Cached - Similar pages

[3] Journal of the American Medical Informatics Association
JAMIA Journal of the American Medical Informaics Association …
refereed papers on the latest developments in the theory and realization of
www.jamia.org/misc/about.html – 23 July 2008 - Cached - Similar pages

[4] [RTF] The University of Exeter - Bioinformatics
File Format: Rich Text Format – View as HTML
This module introduces the **lastest developments** in the fields of genomics …
Research project in the field of bioinformatics and/or **medical informatics** ...
www.biosciences.ex.ac.uk/bioinformatics/module_info.rtf - Cached - Similar pages

[5] BMC Medical Informatics and Decision Making
BMC Medial Informatics and Decision Making is an open access journal publishing original peer-reviewed research articles in information management ...
www.biomedcentral.com/biomedinformeddecismak/index.html 66k

[6] Essential Health Links
... Essential Health Links: Medical Informatics, Telemedicine and E Health journals and digests of latest developments in health informatics ...
www.ehealthlinks.com/links/medical–informatics.html 56k - Cached - Similar pages

[7] [PPT] Medical Informatics Collections
File Format: Microsoft Powerpoint 97 – View as HTML
Medical Informatics and medical librarianship form a strong collecting focus of the National Library of Medicine. Significant **journal** holdings …
www.nlm.nih.gov/hmd/medinfocolls.ppt - Cached - Similar pages

[8] Metropolitan Area Medical Informatics Update
New York City to explore the latest developments in one of the nation's hottest …
healthcare/medical/biomedical informatics with clinical, industrial …
www.cat.columbia.edu/documents/informaticSeminaAnnouncement.html 6 July 2008

[9] [PDF] Guidelines for good evaluation practice and reporting
Incoming chair IMIA working group on Technology Assessment and Quality Development Department of Medical Informatics, Academic Medical Centre, Amsterdam …
lig.umit.at/efmi/mie08/proposal/workshop.pdf 28 March 2008 - Cached - Similar pages

Understanding abbreviations and acronyms

An **abbreviation** is a shorter version of something. For example, PC /piː'siː/ is an abbreviation for *personal computer*.

An **acronym** is similar to an abbreviation, but it is pronounced as a word. For example, PACS /pæks/ is an acronym for *Picture Archiving and Communication System*.

We normally write an abbreviation or acronym with **capital letters**, although the full words have lower case letters. However, there are exceptions, such as www, which is often written with lower case letters.

We **pronounce** the vowel letters in **abbreviations** in this way:

A	/eɪ/
E	/iː/
I	/aɪ/
O	/əʊ/
U	/juː/

We normally **pronounce** the vowel letters in **acronyms** in this way:

A	/æ/
E	/e/
I	/ɪ/
O	/ɒ/
U	/ʌ/

Common suffixes

Suffixes for verbs

Many nouns are made by adding a suffix to a verb. This means:

- you can identify many nouns from the suffix
- you can often discover the verb by removing the suffix (sometimes you have to make changes to the end of the verb)

Examples:

Verb	Suffix	Noun	Notes
amputate	*~ion*	*amputation*	*remove e*
identify	*~ication*	*identification*	*change y to i*
infect	*~tion*	*infection*	
resist	*~nce*	*resistance*	*add a*
treat	*~ment*	*treatment*	
understand	*~ing*	*understanding*	

Developing ideas in a paragraph

Introducing the topic

In a text, a new paragraph indicates the start of a new topic. The topic is given in the **topic sentence**, which is at or near the beginning of the paragraph. The topic sentence gives the **topic** and also makes a **comment** about the topic.

Example:

By the mid-1980s, a new and far more practical approach to medical informatics was becoming possible.

The **topic** is the *more practical approach* which, in this case, concerns medical informatics.

The **comment** is that this *was becoming possible*.

The sentences that follow then expand or explain the topic sentence.

Example:

The fall in the cost of computing power, a result of the development of the PC by IBM in 1980, meant that theoretical research could now be tested in practice.

Developing the topic

A paragraph is normally about the same basic topic (the 'unity' principle). However, within a paragraph, ideas often **develop** beyond the initial comment. This development is often shown by:

* a **discourse marker**: *but, however,* etc.
* a **stance marker**: *unfortunately,* etc.

Examples:

However, during the 1970s, as computers became slightly smaller and less expensive, possibilities for their use in patient care began to be explored.

Unfortunately, while some of these benefits have been realized, the potential of the Internet in telemedicine has yet to be fully exploited.

Discourse markers mainly introduce **contrasts** or **additional information**.

Stance markers show the **attitude** of the writer to the information, i.e., whether he/she is surprised, pleased, unhappy, etc., about the information.

Recording and reporting findings

When you do research, record information about the source. Refer to the source when you report your findings.

Examples:

As McGuire and Pitceathly suggest in their 2002 article in the BMJ, ...

According to Tortora and Grbowski in their book Introduction to the Human Body (2004), ...

You should give the full information about the source in your reference list or bibliography. For more information about this, see Unit 10 *Skills bank*.

5 CAUSES AND EFFECTS OF DISEASE

A
1 Think of the names of three major diseases.
2 Look at the pictures on the opposite page. Name one disease associated with each.

B Study the words in box a.
1 Find pairs of words with similar meanings.
2 What part of speech is each word?

> **a**
> abnormal categories changes detect
> development factors find function groups
> growth happen normal occur reasons
> role unnatural usual variation

C Study the Hadford University handout on this page.
1 Find a word in box a for each blue word or phrase. Change the form if necessary.
2 Find another word in the handout for each red word.

D Study the words in box b.
1 Find pairs of opposites.
2 Add more words to make sets. Name each word set.

> **b**
> active affluent developed female
> healthy male old poor sedentary
> underdeveloped unhealthy young

E
1 Choose a disease from Exercise A. Use words from box b to describe what type of person is likely to get the disease.
2 Your partner should guess which disease you are talking about.

F Look at Figure 1.
1 What does the graph show?
2 What are the projections for each disease?

G Complete the description of Figure 2 opposite.

H Look at Figure 1 again.
1 Which disease will have the greatest reduction in mortality rates between 2005 and 2030?
2 Why do you think this might be?

HADFORD *University*

Faculty: Medicine Studies

Lecture: Causes of disease

Disease occurs when there are variations in the normal structure or function of the body, causing problems or discomfort to the patient.

Disease can be caused by …
- external factors, also called environmental
- internal factors, also called genetic

Diseases can be put into a number of categories:
- inflammatory: where tissue is destroyed by a certain process (e.g., arthritis)
- degenerative: where the normal growth and renewal of tissues does not take place (e.g., Alzheimer's disease)
- neoplastic: where there is abnormal growth in the tissues (e.g., cancer)

Diagnosis takes place when a doctor discovers a disease during examination of a patient and identifies it. It is based on the patient's symptoms, and various tests can be carried out to confirm the diagnosis. Disease can also be detected in regular screenings, such as mammography.

A prediction of the progress of a disease and its likely outcome is known as a *prognosis*.

The graph shows three scenarios for possible changes in the rate of deaths from TB in the world between 1990 and 2020.
In scenario 1, the rate of deaths will _____ _____ from two million in 1990 to one million in 2020, a _____ of one million deaths a year. Scenario 2 suggests that the rate will _____ _____, reaching around 2.2 million by 2020. Scenario 3, the pessimistic scenario, predicts that mortality will _____ to around 3.25 million by 2020. Based on these predictions, the actual rate could either _____ by one million or less or _____ by 1.25 million or less, by 2020.

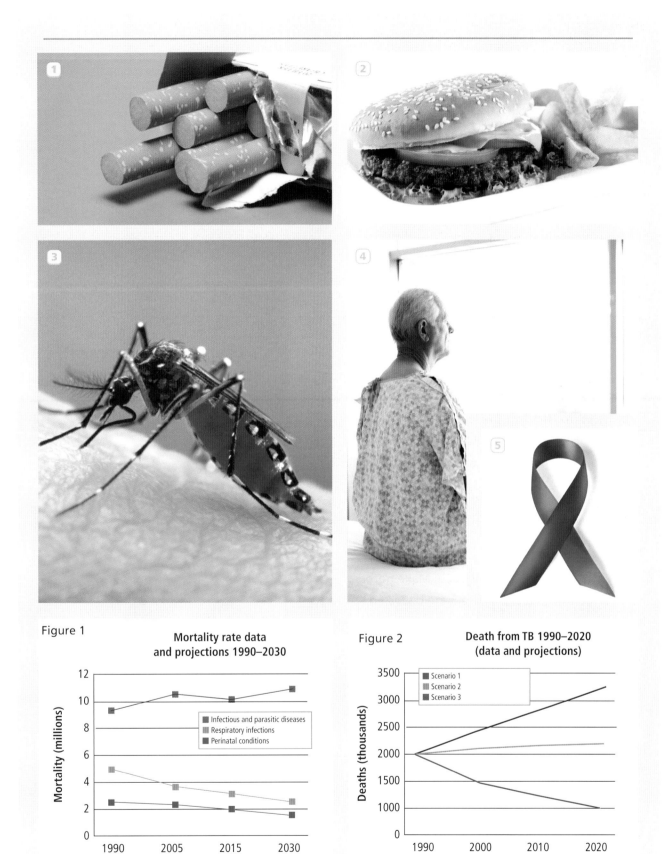

Figure 1

Mortality rate data and projections 1990–2030

■ Infectious and parasitic diseases
■ Respiratory infections
■ Perinatal conditions

Figure 2

Death from TB 1990–2020 (data and projections)

■ Scenario 1
■ Scenario 2
■ Scenario 3

A You are going to hear a lecture about the causes of disease. Look at the lecture slides. What will the lecturer talk about? Make a list of points.

B 🎧 Listen to Part 1 of the lecture. How will the lecture be organized? Number these topics.

- fighting disease   ____
- tools for research   ____
- defining disease   ____
- future projections of disease   ____
- geographical distribution of disease   ____

C Study the topics in Exercise B.

1 Write some key words for each topic.
2 Can you match the topics with slides 1–4?
3 What is a good way to make notes?
4 Make an outline for your notes.

D 🎧 Listen to Part 2 of the lecture.

1 Add information to your outline notes.
2 Which of the topics in Exercise B are discussed? In what order?
3 What are the following examples of?
    a malaria
    b smallpox

E 🎧 Listen to Part 3 of the lecture. Make notes.

1 Which topic(s) in Exercise B are discussed?
2 Give two ways in which we can measure disease levels in a population.
3 What is the lecturer talking about when she loses her place?

F The lecturer used these words and phrases. Match synonyms.

1	be different	extent
2	geography	usefulness
3	find out	important points
4	key concepts	where people live
5	mortality	examination
6	prevalence	identify
7	screening	vary
8	benefits	death

Slide 1

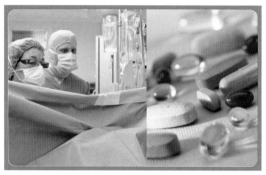

Slide 2

First World
Second World
Third World

Slide 3

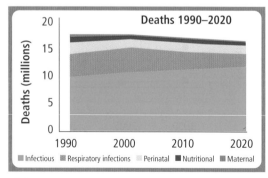

Deaths 1990–2020

Deaths (millions)

20
15
10
5
0

1990   2000   2010   2020

■ Infectious   ■ Respiratory infections   ▪ Perinatal   ■ Nutritional   ■ Maternal

Slide 4

5.3 Extending skills
note-taking symbols • stress within words • lecture language

A Look at the student notes on the right. They are from the lecture in Lesson 5.2.

1 What do the symbols and abbreviations mean?

2 The notes contain some mistakes. Find and correct them.

3 Make the corrected notes into a spidergram.

B 🎧 Listen to the final part of the lecture.

1 Complete your notes.

2 Why does the lecture have to stop?

3 What is the research task?

> 2) diseases by type
>   (i) how get – e.g., cardiac
>   (ii) body part – contagious
> 3) characteristics of population groups
>   (i) demographic, e.g., WHO – s/s
>   Afr AIDS = 1 m (= > 70% wrld)
>   (ii) age – perinatal >1 mth)

C 🎧 Listen to some stressed syllables. Identify the word below in each case. Number each word.

Example: You hear: *1 sem* /sem/

You write:

analyze	____	characteristics	____	seminar	*1*
anticipate	____	identify	____	strategy	____
assignment	____	incredibly	____	successful	____
category	____	overview	____	variety	____

D Study the extract from the lecture on the right.

1 Think of one word for each space.

2 🎧 Listen and check your ideas.

3 Match words or phrases from the blue box below with each word or phrase from the lecture.

4 Think of other words or phrases with similar meanings.

> as I was saying basically clearly
> crucial in fact in other words
> obviously of course possibly
> probably some people say
> that is to say we can see that

E Discuss the research task set by the lecturer.

1 What kind of information should you find?

2 What do you already know?

> _____ , fighting disease is _____ *the* most important aspect of medicine. So, it _____ that it is important to have an excellent knowledge of the characteristics of diseases. What I _____ is their causes and how they can be prevented or cured. Anyway, er … to return to the main _____ – it's _____ to identify population groups. _____ , disease control is about having accurate data on disease levels. _____ , rates of prevalence, incidence and mortality between countries in the developed and developing world can be very different.

A Study the doughnut chart on the opposite page.

1 What does it show?

2 What are communicable diseases and non-communicable conditions? Think of two examples of each.

3 Where do you think the information has come from?

B 🎧 Listen to some extracts from a seminar about research methods.

1 What is wrong with the contribution of the last speaker in each case? Choose from the box, top right.

2 What exactly does the student say in each case?

3 What should the student say or do in each case?

C 🎧 Listen to some more extracts from the same seminar.

1 How does the second speaker make an effective contribution in each case? Choose from the box, right: He/she …

2 What exactly does the student say in each case?

3 What other ways do you know of saying the same things?

D Make a table of **Dos** (helpful ways) and **Don'ts** (unhelpful ways) of contributing to seminar discussions.

Dos	Don'ts
ask politely for information	demand information from other students

- It is irrelevant.
- The student doesn't contribute anything to the discussion.
- The student interrupts.
- It is not polite.
- The student doesn't explain the relevance.

- brings the discussion back to the main point
- brings in another speaker
- asks for clarification
- links when not sure the contribution is new
- paraphrases to check understanding
- gives specific examples to explain a point
- links when not sure the contribution is relevant
- disagrees politely with a previous speaker
- links to a previous speaker

E Work in groups.

1 The teacher will ask you to look at the data for disease group A (communicable diseases) or B (non-communicable conditions) in Figure 2 on the opposite page. The data shows mortality from diseases in each group for four different countries.

2 From the data and your knowledge of the diseases, for each of the countries A, B, C and D, think of a real country which might have a similar mortality profile.

3 What words do you think could be used to describe the countries?

4 What reasons do you think there may be for the difference in mortality rates for each disease in each of the countries? Outline your reasons to the group, using the statistics which best support your argument.

5 Conduct a seminar. One person should act as observer.

F Report on your discussion and present your reasons using supporting statistics.

G Work in groups of four. Each person should research and discuss one of the four main types of research. The teacher will give you a discussion task card with more instructions.

- Student A: find out about secondary research (information on page 103)
- Student B: find out about primary research (information on page 103)
- Student C: find out about qualitative research (information on page 104)
- Student D: find out about quantitative research (information on page 104)

Figure 1: *Mortality rates by type (%)*

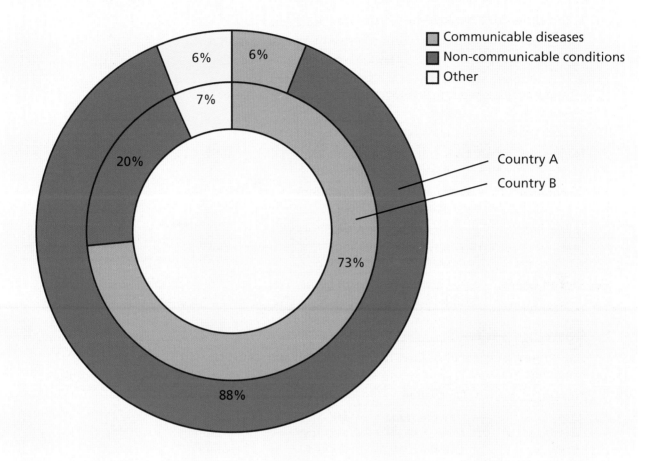

Figure 2: *Mortality rates by type and country (per thousand people)*

	Country A	Country B	Country C	Country D
A Communicable diseases				
Tuberculosis	3.4	0.0	0.1	3.9
HIV/AIDS	26.9	0.5	0.2	1.2
Childhood diseases	3.7	0.0	0.0	4.4
Malaria	9.6	0.0	0.0	1.6
B Non-communicable conditions	19.7	87.5	89.0	44.4
Malignant neoplasms	3.6	23.6	26.5	5.7
Diabetes mellitus	0.7	3.1	2.4	1.2
Cardiovascular diseases	9.0	37.9	41.1	23.1
Respiratory diseases	2.2	7.3	5.6	3.7

Vocabulary sets

It is a good idea to learn words which go together. Why?

- It is easier to remember the words.
- You will have alternative words to use when paraphrasing research findings.
- It is not good style to repeat the same word often, so writers, and sometimes speakers, make use of words from the same set to avoid repetition.

You can create a vocabulary set with:

synonyms	words with similar meanings, e.g., *disease/condition/illness*
antonyms	words with opposite meanings, e.g., *male/female*
hypernyms	a general word for a set of words, e.g., *diseases = infectious, congenital, hereditary,* etc.
linked words	e.g., *young, teenage, in his/her 20s, middle-aged, old*

Describing trends

You can use a variety of phrases to discuss trends and statistics.
Examples:

Go up	No change	Go down	Adverbs
rise	*stay the same*	*fall*	*slightly*
increase	*remain at …*	*decrease*	*gradually*
grow	*doesn't change*	*decline*	*steadily*
improve	*is unchanged*	*worsen*	*significantly*
soar		*drop*	*sharply*
		plunge	*dramatically*
		plummet	

Stance

Speakers often use certain words and phrases to show how they feel about what they are saying.
Common stance words are:

adverbs	*arguably* *naturally* *unfortunately*
phrases	*of course, …* *it's essential to/that …* *we might say that …*

In many cases, different stance words and phrases are used in spoken and written language.

Spoken	Written
another thing	*additionally*
it seems	*evidently*
unfortunately	*regrettably*
believe	*contend*

Signpost language in a lecture

At the beginning of a lecture, a speaker will usually outline the talk. To help listeners understand the order of topics, the speaker will use phrases such as:

To start with *I'll talk about …*   **After that**, *we'll look at …*
Then *I'll discuss …*   **I'll finish by** *giving a summary of …*

During the lecture, the speaker may:

indicate a new topic	*Moving on (from this) …*
say the same thing in a different way	*What I mean is, …* *That is to say, …* *To put it another way, …*
return to the main point	*Where was I? Oh, yes.* *To return to the main point …* *As I was saying …*

Seminar language

The discussion leader may:

ask for information	*What did you learn about …?* *Can you explain …?* *Can you tell me a bit more about …?*
ask for opinions	*What do you make of …?* *This is interesting, isn't it?*
bring in other speakers	*What do you think, Tomas?* *What's your opinion, Evie?*

Participants should:

be polite when disagreeing	*Actually, I don't quite agree …*
make relevant contributions	*That reminds me …*
give examples to explain a point	*I can give an example of that.*

Participants may:

agree with the previous speaker	*I agree, and that's why …* *That's true, so I think …* *You're absolutely right, which is why …*
disagree with the previous speaker	*I don't think I agree with that.* *In my opinion, …* *I'm not sure that's true. I think …*
link to a previous speaker	*As Jack said earlier, …* *Going back to what Leila said …*
ask for clarification	*Could you say more about …?*
paraphrase to check understanding	*So what you're saying is …*
refer back to establish relevance	*Just going back to …*

Participants may not be sure if a contribution is new or relevant:
I'm sorry. Has anybody made the point that …?
I don't know if this is relevant.

6 BIOLOGY, BIOCHEMISTRY AND PHARMACOLOGY

A Study the words in the blue box.

  1 Copy and complete the table. Put the words in one or more columns in each case.

  2 Add or remove affixes to make words for the empty boxes. (Some will not be possible.)

  3 What is the meaning of each term?

  4 Find a synonym for each word.

  5 Group the words in the blue box according to their stress pattern.

B Study Figures 1a and 1b on the opposite page. Discuss these questions using words from Exercise A.

  1 What do the diagrams show?

  2 What does the diagram show about the similarities and differences between human cells, bacteria and viruses?

  3 What does Figure 1b show?

C Student A has written about the cell reproduction cycle in Figure 1b, but there are some mistakes. Change the blue words so that the sentences are true.

D Student B has also written about the cell reproduction cycle. Match each sentence with a corrected sentence from Exercise C.

E Look at Figure 2 on the opposite page.

  1 What does it show?

  2 Match the descriptions below the figure to the correct stage.

  3 Rewrite one of the descriptions in your own words. Give your sentence to your partner. Your partner should guess which stage you have described.

  4 Rewrite the descriptions of the other three stages.

---

analysis	anatomical	cell
characteristics	contaminants	convert
cycle daughter	destruction	envelope
equatorial generalized		identify
infection instructions		metabolic
nucleus prevent		replication
separation sign		specialized

Noun	Verb	Adjective
Infection	Infect	Infectious

Student A

1. The nuclear envelope *develops* during the prophase

2. The number of chromosomes in the cell *halves* during the prophase

3. In the metaphase, the chromosomes *scatter* at the equator of the cell

4. During the anaphase, the chromosomes *join*

5. During the telophase, the nuclear envelope begins to gradually *disappear*

6. The two new cells created in the cycle are *mother* cells of the original cell

Student B

a. As the telophase progresses, the nuclear envelope reappears gradually

b. During the prophase, the nuclear envelope begins to break down

c. In the first part of the reproductive cycle, the number of chromosomes in the cell doubles

d. Separation of the chromosomes occurs during the anaphase

e. The product of the cycle is two daughter cells which have been created from the original cell

f. The chromosomes align themselves in the equator of the cell in the metaphase

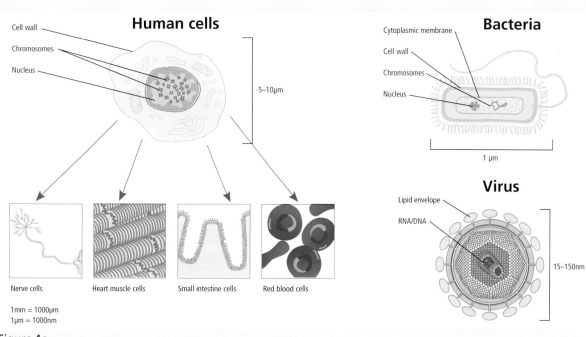

Figure 1a

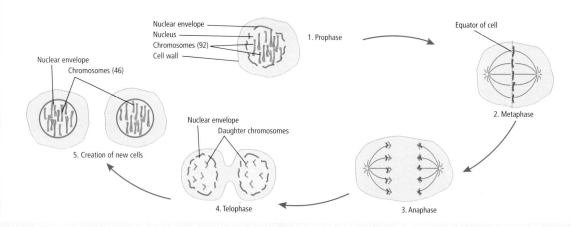

Figure 1b

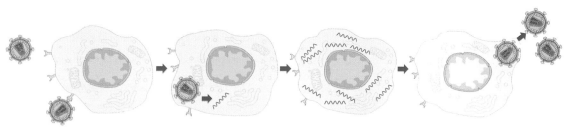

a) Cell material converted into new viruses, destroying cell in the process

b) Virus infects the cell, injecting DNA through cell membrane

c) Virus attaches to cell

d) Virus DNA replicates itself using cell mechanisms

Figure 2

A Study the picture opposite.

   1 What is being shown in the picture?

   2 What significance might this have in medicine today?

B Discuss these questions.

   1 List some everyday products or plants that have been used for medicinal purposes in the past.

   2 What have they been used for?

   3 Name the discipline related to the study of drugs and medication.

C Look at the pictures, the title, the introduction and the first sentence of each paragraph on the opposite page.

   1 What will the text be about?

   2 Using your ideas from Exercises A, B and C1, write some research questions.

D Read the text. Does it answer your questions?

E Study the highlighted sentences in the text. Find and underline the subject, verb and object or complement in each sentence. *See Skills bank.*

F Two students paraphrased part of the text.

   1 Which parts of the text are these paraphrases of?

   2 Which paraphrase is better? Why?

G Work in groups. Write a paraphrase of a different part of the text. *See Vocabulary bank.*

Student A

Information about these plants was passed from generation to generation and is the source of much of our knowledge today.

The South American Indians gave us the first relaxant: curare, which they put onto their spears to paralyze animals when they hunted.

A drug that has the same properties is used by surgeons today to relax patients during medical interventions.

A second example is cocaine, which was written about early on and was described as a product with important effects on the body.

Student B

Much of the information that pharmacologists possess today about the medicinal properties of plants has been passed down through generations.

The first muscle relaxant, curare, originated with the indigenous population of South America, a hunting people who used it to paralyze their prey.

These days, patients going into surgery are given a drug with similar properties to relax their muscles.

Early entries on cocaine can be found, highlighting its uses and effects on the body.

Principles of pharmacology

An understanding of the principles of pharmacology forms a key component in the study of medicine. From the Greek *pharmakon*, pharmacology is the branch of medical science that deals with the mechanism of actions, uses, harmful effects and outcomes of drugs on animals and humans. It examines the way in which drugs produce both beneficial and adverse side effects on the body.

Students of pharmacology look at the way in which the biochemical, physiological and psychological processes in health and disease are affected by drugs. When we talk about drugs, we are referring to biologically active compounds that change the state of the functioning of the body and improve health in some way – by relieving pain, calming the patient or eliminating infection, for example. We are also concerned with enhancing the way in which drugs are tested, so that they can eventually give greater benefit in the treatment of disease.

There are several types of pharmacology, and it is possible to divide the discipline into four distinct areas. Firstly, there is *autonomic pharmacology*, which is the study of the effect of chemicals and drugs on the functioning of the autonomic nervous system. This area also covers studies on other parts of the nervous system, including the central nervous system. The study of the molecular structure of internal receptors and the design of drug molecules to interact with specific receptor areas is known as *molecular pharmacology*, while *biochemical pharmacology* is the study of the effects of chemicals on the biochemical processes associated with the functioning of cells. The fourth and final area of the discipline is *toxicology*, which looks at the adverse effects of chemicals on the body, the side effects of drugs and the effects of environmental contaminants on the body.

Because pharmacology involves examination of the effects of chemicals on biological systems on a number of different levels, there is a clear link between biochemistry and pharmacology. For example, drugs and poisons usually act by interfering with specific metabolic pathways. Antibiotic penicillin is a good example of the effects of chemicals on biological systems, as it destroys bacteria by inhibiting an enzyme that synthesizes an essential polysaccharide of the bacterial wall.

Pharmacology as a scientific discipline dates from the mid-1800s, but its development has taken place over many centuries and has been influenced by many different cultures. The discovery of many drugs and medicinal plants was largely through trial and error. Across the world as tribal man foraged for food, he soon realized that his local woodland areas harboured a variety of roots, barks, berries and leaves which were not only sources of food, but also in some cases possessed medicinal (healing, soothing and therapeutic) properties. He also came across other matters that were highly toxic. Information about such plants was handed down from generation to generation, providing the basis of much of our knowledge today. One such example is the South American Indians, who gave us the first muscle relaxant: a drug called curare that they smeared onto the tips of their spears to immobilize animals when hunting. Today a drug which possesses similar characteristics is used by doctors to relax their patients' muscles during surgery. Another is cocaine, which is documented very early on as being a substance with profound effects on the human body; it is a stimulant of the central nervous system and was used as an appetite suppressant, an analgesic and an anaesthetic.

So what does the future hold for contemporary pharmacology? Having made significant advances in the field, researchers have now created so-called 'designer drugs'. This is done by modifying the chemical structure of an existing drug. There is also a greater understanding of the molecular structures of viruses and as a result biochemists are now able to design antiviral agents. Both discoveries are sure to have far-reaching consequences for the future of medicine.

A Study the words in box a from the text in Lesson 6.2.

  1 What part of speech are they in the text?

  2 Find one or more words in the text with a similar meaning to each word.

B Complete the summary with words from Exercise A. You may need to change the form of the words.

C Study the words in box b.

  1 What is each base word and its meaning?

  2 How does the affix change the part of speech?

  3 What is the meaning in the text in Lesson 6.2?

D Study sentences A–E on the opposite page.

  1 Copy and complete Table 1. Put the parts of each sentence in the correct column.

  2 Rewrite the main part of each sentence, changing the verb from active to passive or vice versa.

E Look at the 'Other verbs' column in Table 1.

  1 How are the clauses linked to the main part of the sentence?

  2 In sentences A, B and D, what does each relative pronoun refer to?

  3 Make the clauses into complete sentences.

a

eliminate   adverse   soothing
therapeutic   toxic
characteristics   substance

Pharmacology is essentially the study of drugs. Drugs are _____ that are both _____ and beneficial, with different _____ that react on the human body. Some drugs might be used in the treatment of certain diseases, for example _____ infection, while others are _____, _____ and relieve the patient's symptoms. However, some drugs can have quite _____ effects on the human body. Such drugs are the subject of the study of toxicology, which also takes into consideration the effect of contaminants from the patient's environment.

b

beneficial   biochemical
functioning   molecular   interact
scientific   relaxant
immobilize   antiviral

A Make one sentence for each box on the right, using the method given in red. Include the words in blue. Write all the sentences as one paragraph.

B Study the notes on the opposite page which a student has made about another example from the history of pharmacology.

  1 Divide the notes into sections to make suitable paragraphs.

  2 Decide which ideas are suitable topic sentences for the paragraphs.

  3 Make full sentences from the notes, joining ideas where possible, to make one continuous text.

The Sumerians compiled the first medical 'handbook'. This 'handbook' listed symptoms of illnesses.
relative, passive   5,000 years ago

It included prescriptions for medicinal plants used for the treatment of symptoms. It included animal parts used for the treatment of symptoms.
passive, ellipsis   In the 'handbook'

The Ancient Egyptians developed complex theories to explain the causes of disease. These theories highlighted the treatment of disease.
relative, passive, ellipsis   Later

The ancient remedies combined physical effects such as inducing drowsiness with the belief they could drive out evil spirits. We learn that the Ancient Egyptians believed sickness derived from the supernatural.
participle   As a result

A Today, a drug which possesses similar characteristics is used by doctors to relax their patients' muscles during surgery.

B **Students of pharmacology look at the way in which the biochemical, physiological and psychological processes in health and disease are affected by drugs.**

C It is possible to divide the discipline into four distinct areas.

D **The fourth and final area of the discipline is toxicology, which looks at the adverse effects of chemicals on the body.**

E Information about such plants was handed down from generation to generation, providing the basis for much of our knowledge today.

Table 1: Breaking a complex sentence into constituent parts

	Main S	Main V	Main O/C	Other V + S/O/C	Adv. phrases
A	a drug	is used	by doctors	¹which possesses similar characteristics ²to relax their patients' muscles during surgery	Today
B					

Medicinal plant: ginseng = 1 of best e.g.s
- ginseng ft root = resembles human figure
- used in Chinese medicine - 1,000s yrs
- sweet + faint aroma
- known as 'root of life'
- + medicinal props
- adapts to human system - combats neg. conditions, e.g. stress/malnutrition/ageing
- Traditionally Chinese belief = ginseng balance yin + yang in body + Native American women: e.g. = – menstrual probs
- e.g.s of > 25 medical problems used:
  - anaemia
  - indigestion
  - impotence
  - depression
  - sleep patterns
  - increase energy
- Other points – remember =
  - + slight bitter taste
  - metal → destroy healing props
  - therefore prepare in earthenware
  - avoid + caffeine / stimulants → irritable
- today still used
- find – health stores across world
- buy in different forms:
  - dried ʸ herbal tea
  - whole
  - sliced
  - energy drink
- However, bear in mind - some - reactions
- Side effects < + longer to emerge/conventional meds = rash / nausea + headaches (= rare) → ↓dosage. If s.e. contin. discontin.

Reporting findings

You cannot use another writer's words unless you directly quote. Instead, you must restate or **paraphrase**.

There are several useful ways to do this:

use a synonym of a word or phrase	relieve → ease in the beginning → early in the cycle
change negative to positive and vice versa	the treatment alleviated the symptoms → the treatment didn't exacerbate the symptoms
use a replacement subject	symptoms may improve → there may be an improvement in the symptoms
change from active to passive or vice versa	the lotion can sooth the itching → the itching can be soothed by the lotion
change the order of information	in the beginning, the drug had adverse side effects → there were adverse side effects early on in the cycle

When reporting findings from one source, you should use all the methods above.

Example:

Original text	The number of chromosomes in the cell doubles during the prophase.
Report	In the prophase, there are twice as many chromosomes in the cell compared with the normal number.

Important

When paraphrasing, you should aim to make sure that 90% of the words you use are different from the original. It is not enough to change only a few vocabulary items: this will result in plagiarism. A paraphrase should only be used in conjunction with a clear acknowledgement of the source.

Example:

Original text	The product of the cycle is two daughter cells which have been created from the original cell.
Plagiarism	The result of the cycle is the creation of two daughter cells from the original cell.

Finding the main information

Sentences in academic and technical texts are often very long.

Example:
*Following the discovery of the role of DNA (deoxyribonucleic acid) in cell replication, **scientists** looking at DNA's role in controlling this process were able to automatically **make** the **link** between chemistry and biology much clearer, allowing them to carry out even more detailed analysis.*

You often don't have to understand every word, but you must **identify the subject**, **the verb and the object**, if there is one.

For example, in the sentence above, we find:
subject = *scientists*
verb = *make*
object = *link*

Remember!

You can remove any leading prepositional phrases at this point to help you find the subject, e.g., *Following the discovery …*

You must then find **the main words which modify** the subject, the verb and the object or complement.

In the sentence above, we find:
***Which** scientists*? = those researching DNA's role in controlling cell replication
***How** make*? = automatically
***What** link*? = the one between chemistry and biology

Ellipsis

Sometimes, if the meaning is clear, words are implied rather than actually given in the text.

Examples:
Clinical pathology is the branch of pathology (that is) concerned with the technical and theoretical aspects of identifying disease in the laboratory.

It was possible to gain a better understanding of the effects of disease on the individual cells and (the effects of disease) on the body as a whole.

7.1 Vocabulary   compound nouns • fixed phrases

A Study the words in box a.

  1 Match nouns in column 1 with nouns in column 2 to make compound nouns.

  2 Which word in each phrase has the strongest stress?

B Study the phrases in box b.

  1 Complete each phrase with one word.

  2 Is each phrase followed by:
- a noun (including gerund)?
- subject + verb?
- an infinitive?

  3 What is each phrase used for?

C Look at the pictures from a patient leaflet on the opposite page, showing a journey through A&E. What happens at each stage?

D Read extracts A–F on the right.

  1 Match each extract with a picture on the opposite page.

  2 Complete each sentence with one or more phrases from box b.

E Look at the chart on the opposite page. What does it show?

F Read the text under the chart. Match the phrases in box c with the highlighted phrases in the handout.

G Complete the memo below regarding an Integrated Care Pathway for Patient X using phrases from boxes b and c.

Our decision regarding the Integrated Care Pathway we recommend for Patient X is _____ a number of factors. Patient satisfaction ratings, _____ the feedback, were very strongly in favour of option 2. However, we have to _____ that _____ some of our practitioners, this is not the best option. _____ those who have used it in draft form, the feedback has been mostly negative. _____ this, increased cost has been a factor.

1	2
case recovery	symptoms room
disease human	nurse department
physiotherapy	body care notes
triage emergency	

b

as shown …   as well …   in addition …

in order …   in such a way …

in the case …   known …   the end …

the use …

A Before the operation, _____ gaining informed consent from the patient, the consultant will need to explain the procedure in detail.

B Post-operation patients on the orthopaedic ward will have their vital signs recorded hourly, exactly _____ the monitor. After 24 hours, the number on the monitor can be rounded to one decimal place.

C After discharge, an appointment should be offered to attend the outpatient's clinic, _____ as the physiotherapy department.

D Patients with a suspected fracture should be transferred to the X-ray department, _____ determine whether a break has occurred. The _____ a wheelchair or stretcher is obligatory, and the transfer should be handled _____ pain to the patient is minimized.

E _____ a patient classified as a priority case by a specialist nurse _____ a triage nurse, the senior doctor on duty must be notified as soon as possible and the patient admitted to Accident & Emergency.

F At _____ the operation, the operating equipment should be checked carefully, before moving the patient to the recovery room.

c

a number of   a variety of

at the same time   bear in mind

based on   deal with

from the point of view of

the beginning of   the development of

Harold is admitted to Accident & Emergency (A&E) with a suspected fractured hip. Here is his journey.

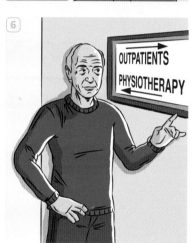

Integrated Care Pathway

	Week 1	Week 2	Week 3	Week 4	Week 5	Week 6	Week 7
Working Group decide priorities for ICP implementations	■						
Clinicians discuss initial choices with colleagues	■						
Number of draft ICPs created		■	■				
Decision on which ICPs will be piloted				■			
Pilot implementation of ICP by clinicians					■	■	■
Collection of feedback from patients					■	■	■
Final decision on full implementation of ICPs							

The Gantt chart above shows the evolution of an Integrated Care Pathway (ICP), which sets out in detail the stages of care, diagnosis and treatment of specific illnesses. With regards to the hospital, ICPs make it easier to handle situations where different departments are responsible for delivering care. The start of the process involves setting up a Working Group, made up of several clinical and management representatives. They discuss priorities for the development of the ICPs in the hospital and use various criteria to help them decide. Simultaneously, the clinicians discuss the practical implications of the ICPs with their staff and, using their feedback, identify several possible options, which are developed in draft form. Feedback from patients and clinicians is then used to make a final decision on which ICPs provide the greatest benefit and will be fully implemented.

A You are going to hear the lecture outlined on the slide. Write four questions you would like answered.

B 🎧 Listen to Part 1 of the lecture.

   1 What is the lecturer going to talk about today? Write *yes*, *no* or *not mentioned*.

      • emergency care _____   • primary care _____

      • palliative care _____   • care cycle _____

      • patient journey _____

      • problems in provision of hospital care _____

   2 What is *acute care*?

C 🎧 Listen to Part 2 of the lecture.

   1 Make notes in an appropriate form.

   2 Roughly what percentage of patients enter hospital for emergency treatment?

   3 What is specific about doctors working in acute care departments? Give some examples.

   4 Were your questions in Exercise A answered?

D Match each fixed phrase in the table on the right with the type of information that can follow.

E 🎧 Listen to Part 3 of the lecture.

   1 Make notes after the phrases in Exercise D.

   2 Were your questions in Exercise A answered?

F 🎧 Listen for sentences 1–3 in Part 4 of the lecture. Which sentence (**a** or **b**) follows in each case? Why? *See Skills bank.*

   1 Promotions and prevention is our first stage.
     a In the promotions and prevention stage, the difference is that it can be carried out on two levels simultaneously.
     b What's different about the promotions and prevention stage is that it can be carried out on two levels simultaneously.

   2 Stage four of our generic cycle is the management stage.
     a In this stage of the cycle, stabilizing the patient and continuing with the prescribed treatment is of utmost importance.
     b Stabilizing the patient and continuing the prescribed treatment is of utmost importance in this stage of the cycle.

   3 Lastly, there is rehabilitation.
     a In this stage, the important feature is that by the end of it the patient is able to function in his or her normal environment again.
     b What's important about this stage is that by the end of it, the patient is once again able to function in his or her normal environment.

G This lecturer is not very well organized. What problems are there in the lecture?

HADFORD *University*

Acute care (Lecture 1)

Lecture overview

• Definition of acute care

• Patient journey

• Integrated Care Pathway

• Care cycle

Fixed phrase	Followed by ...
1 An important concept (is) ...	a different way to think about the topic
2 What do I mean by ...?	an imaginary example
3 As you can see, ...	a key statement or idea
4 Say ...	a concluding comment giving a result of something
5 Looking at it another way, ...	a new idea or topic that the lecturer wants to discuss
6 The point is ...	a comment about a diagram or picture
7 In financial terms, ...	an explanation of a word or phrase
8 In this way, ...	a general idea put into a financial context

7.3 Extending skills
stress within words • fixed phrases • giving sentences a special focus

A 🎧 Listen to some stressed syllables. Identify the word below in each case. Number each word.

Example:

You hear: *1 cute* /kjuːt/

You write:

accredited	___	diagnosis	___	prevention	___
acute	I	discharge	___	promotion	___
admission	___	emergency	___	rehabilitation	___
behavioural	___	initiated	___	simultaneously	___

B 🎧 Listen to the final part of the lecture from Lesson 7.2.

1 Complete the notes on the right by adding a symbol in each space.

2 What research task(s) are you asked to do?

C Study the phrases from the lecture in the blue box. For which of the following purposes did the lecturer use each phrase?

- to introduce a new topic
- to emphasize a major point
- to add points
- to finish a list
- to give an example
- to restate

D Rewrite these sentences to give a special focus. Begin with the words in brackets.

1 Dr DeWitt Mills established a system of 24-hour care. (*It*)

2 The 'Alexandria Plan' meant that the US media and various health reports published at the time were able to highlight the poor state of training in this particular field. (*The result*)

3 The American Board of Medical Specialities finally recognized EM as a medical speciality in 1979. (*It*)

4 Improving acute care provision is really important for the future of many national health care systems today. (*What*)

See *Skills bank.*

E Choose one section of the lecture. Refer to your notes and give a spoken summary. Use the fixed phrases and ways of giving special focus that you have looked at.

F Work with a partner.

1 Prepare a patient journey for a patient presenting to A&E with a specific condition. (You may choose the condition.)

2 Present your patient journey to another pair. Practise using fixed phrases and ways of giving special focus.

See *Vocabulary bank and Skills bank.*

EM – when start?

Dewitt Mills _____ 'Alexandria Plan' – 1960s

> *_____ 'AP': Probs:*
>
> *1   EM run by specialists on rotation*
>
> *2   interns (training) – nurses called on*
>
> *3   ER poorly organized _____ no specific training*
>
> *_____ 'AP' → media + reports _____ level training in EDs in US*

1970 Cincinnati H. _____ 1st EM doc

EM recognized 1979 as specialty in medical field

> et cetera
> In other words, …
> Let's take …
> Let me put it another way.
> Not to mention the fact that …
> Plus there's the fact that …
> The fact of the matter is, …
> You've probably heard of …

A Look at the web page and the photographs on the opposite page.

   1 What do they show?

   2 How is the care or advice being provided?

B 🎧 Listen to the first extract from a seminar about ways to improve acute care provision.

   1 What question will the students discuss?

   2 How does the lecturer think acute care provision will change in the future?

C 🎧 Listen to Part 2 of the seminar. Are these sentences true or false?

   1 If minor injuries can be dealt with elsewhere, Emergency Departments can focus on more complex cases.

   2 The hospital is not always the best place for the patient.

   3 Nurses are getting paid for carrying out the duties of a doctor.

   4 The role of nurses is a key issue in improving emergency care.

   5 Even if 'patient flow' is improved, waiting times will still be long.

D Study a–d below and the phrases in the blue box.

   1 Write **a**, **b**, **c** or **d** next to each phrase to show its use.
     a introducing
     b asking for clarification
     c agreeing/disagreeing
     d clarifying

   2 🎧 Listen to Part 2 again to check your answers.

E Work in groups of four to research the main ways to improve acute care provision in Emergency Departments. Each person should choose a different criterion.

  • Student A: Read about *specialist centres* on page 105.

  • Student B: Read about *minor injuries units* on page 105.

  • Student C: Read about *cycle paramedics* on page 106.

  • Student D: Read about *air ambulance services* on page 106.

After reading the notes, report back orally to your group.
Use fixed phrases to ask for and give clarification.

F Work in groups. Choose one of the ways of improving acute care provision shown in the photographs.

   1 Have a practice seminar in which you decide on the best alternative to the current acute care situation.

   2 Report to the class on your discussion, giving reasons for your decisions.

Retrieved January 15, 2010 from NHS Direct website:
http://www.nhsdirect.nhs.uk

I'd like to make two points. First, … ___
Can you expand on that? ___
The point is … ___
What's your second point? ___
My second point is that … ___
Yes, but … ___
I don't agree with that because … ___
Sorry, but what are we talking about exactly? ___
We need to be clear here. ___
I'd just like to say that … ___
In what way? ___
What I'm trying to say is … ___
Can you give me an example? ___
Look at it this way. ___
Absolutely. ___

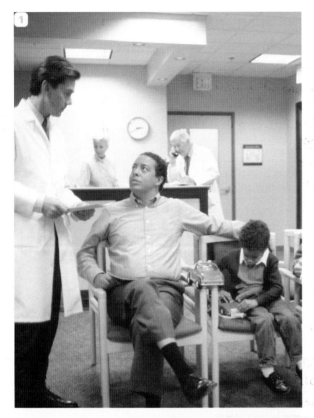

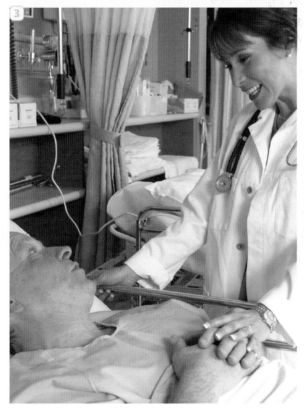

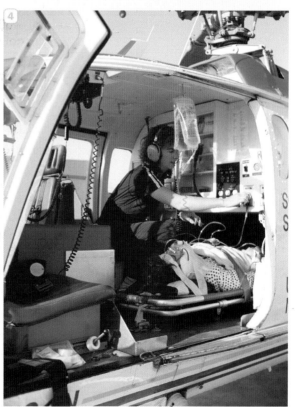

Recognizing fixed phrases from medical studies (1)

There are many fixed phrases in the field of medical studies.

Examples:

Phrase	Meaning in the discipline
acute care	the treatment of a disease or symptoms that requires immediate attention, emergency care
patient admissions	where a patient is registered on entering hospital
triage nurse	nurse who assesses and prioritizes cases for treatment in the Emergency Department of a hospital
vital signs	bodily systems that are essential for life, e.g., heartbeat, body temperature, breathing

Keep a list of fixed phrases used in medical studies and remind yourself regularly of the meaning.

Recognizing fixed phrases from academic English (1)

There are also a large number of fixed phrases which are commonly used in academic and technical English in general.

Examples:

Phrase	What comes next?
As we have seen, …	a reminder of previous information
An important concept is …	one of the basic points underlying the topic
As you can see, …	a reference to an illustration OR a logical conclusion from previous information
As shown in …	a reference to a diagram or table
… in such a way that …	a result of something
In addition to (X, Y) *As well as (X, Y)*	X = reminder of last point, Y = new point
In the case of …	a reference to a particular topic or, more often, sub-topic
At the same time, …	an action or idea which must be considered alongside another action or idea
… based on …	a piece of research, a theory, an idea
Bear in mind (that) …	key information which helps to explain (or limit in some way) previous information
The point is …	the basic information underlying an explanation
in order to (do X, Y)	X = objective, Y = necessary actions/conditions
In medical terms, …	related to something medical previously mentioned
In other words, … *Looking at it another way, …*	the same information put in a different way
In this way, …	a result from previous information
Say …	an example
What do I mean by (X)?	an explanation of X

Make sure you know what kind of information comes next.

Skills bank

'Given' and 'new' information in sentences

In English, we can put important information at the beginning or at the end of a sentence. There are two types of important information.

1 Information which the listener or reader already knows from general knowledge or from previous information in the text. This can be called 'given' information. It normally goes at the beginning of the sentence.

2 Information which is new in this text. This can be called 'new' information. It normally goes at the end of a sentence.

Example:

In Lesson 7.2, the lecturer is talking about patient flow, so patient flow in general = given information.

Given	New
Stage four of our generic cycle	*is the management stage.*
In this stage of the cycle,	*stabilizing the patient is of utmost importance.*

Giving sentences a special focus

We sometimes change the normal word order to emphasize a particular point, e.g., a person, an object, a time.

Examples:

Normal sentence	*Dr DeWitt Mills established a system of 24-hour care in the 1960s.*
Focusing on person	*It was Dr DeWitt Mills who established ...*
Focusing on object	*It was the system of 24-hour care which Dr DeWitt Mills established ...*
Focusing on time	*It was in the 1960s that Dr DeWitt Mills ...*

Introducing new information

We can use special structures to introduce a new topic.

Examples:

Acute care is my subject today.
  ➔ **What I am going to talk about today is** *acute care.*

The patient is very important.
  ➔ **What is very important is** *the patient.*

Increased numbers using A&E cause the problem.
  ➔ **The reason for the problem is** *an increase in the numbers using A&E.*

A poor 'patient flow' leads to longer waiting times.
  ➔ **The result of poor 'patient flow' is** *longer waiting times.*

Clarifying points

When we are speaking, we often have to clarify points. There are many expressions which we can use.

Examples:

Let me put it another way.   *What I'm trying to say is ...*
Look at it this way, ...   *The point/thing is ...*

8.1 Vocabulary — synonyms • nouns from verbs • paraphrasing

A Discuss the following questions.

1 What is meant by *primary care*?

2 Each of the words in box a is associated with a type of clinic. What benefits do you think each of the clinics provides?

B Using pictures A–E and the staff list, match the picture with the occupation.

C Look up each noun in box b in a dictionary.

1 Is it countable, uncountable or both?

2 What is its meaning in medicine?

3 What is a good synonym?

4 What useful grammatical information can you find?

D Study the two lists of verbs in box c.

1 Match the verbs with similar meanings.

2 Make nouns from the verbs if possible.

E Look at the Hadford University handout.

1 How does the writer restate each section heading in the paragraph?

2 Find synonyms for the blue words and phrases. Use a dictionary if necessary.

3 Rewrite each sentence to make paraphrases of the texts. Use:

- synonyms you have found yourself
- synonyms from Exercise C
- the nouns you made in Exercise D
- passives where possible
- any other words that are necessary

Example:

A major preventative role of primary care is to help patients avoid disease or disability.

→ *Primary care has a major role in assisting patients to avoid illness or disability.*

F Choose one of the occupations from the staff list and list five words which could be used as part of their job description. Use some words from box c if possible.

---

a

ante/postnatal foot pain
weight smoking

b

ailment allergy analgesic clinic
concern fatigue illness injection
nausea pain pill vaccination

c

1	2
advise	verify
assess	outline
check	update
detect	reduce
examine	evaluate
explain	find
help	transfer
manage	look at
minimize	sympathize
refer	assist
renew	recommend
support	control

HADFORD *University*

The role of primary care

A Preventative medicine

A major preventative role of primary care is to help patients avoid disease or disability. It is, perhaps, even more crucial than its other role, providing treatment for patients who suffer from these conditions already. An important aspect of this is the vaccination services that the clinics provide.

B Support for acute care

The support role of primary care is to detect disease at an early stage and to refer patients to acute care for further tests or treatments. This means that the damage caused by a disease can be minimized. It can also help with monitoring the progress of post-operative healing, so complications can be identified quickly.

SURGERY STAFF

General Practitioners – **Dr Mike Brown**
BSC MB BS MRCGP
Dr Maria Archer MRCS
MB BS LRCP MRCGP DRCOG
Dr Frances Green MB BS
DCH DFFP
Practice Nurses – **Sr Megan Wilde**
Sr Julie French
Practice Manager – **Peter Read**
Receptionists – **Beryl Cook**
Samantha Pottinger
Dietician – **Prudence Smith**
Podiatrist – **Ellen Finch**
Physiotherapist – **Jane Airey** MCSP, BSc (Hons)

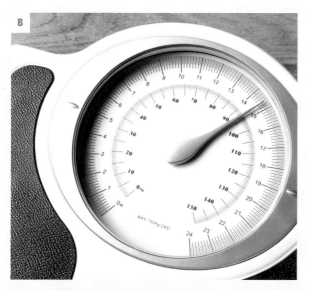

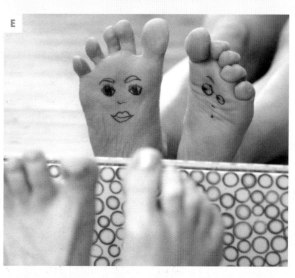

A Look at the conditions in the blue box.

1 Which are best managed in primary care and which will need to be referred to acute care?

2 Which conditions could primary care help prevent?

3 Which conditions are suitable for follow-up in primary care?

B Look at the four essay types on the right.

1 What should the writer do in each type?

2 Match each essay type with one of the questions below the slide (A–D).

3 What topics should be covered in each essay question?

C Read the title of the text on the opposite page and the first sentence of each paragraph.

1 What will the text be about?

2 Choose one of the essay questions in Exercise B. Write four research questions which will help you to find information for your essay.

D Read the text.

1 Using your own words, make notes from the text on information for your essay question.

2 Work with another person who has chosen the same essay question as you. Compare your notes.

E Study the highlighted sentences in the text.

1 Underline all the subjects and their verbs.

2 Which is the main subject and verb for each sentence?

F Study the table on the right.

1 Match each word or phrase with its meaning.

2 Underline the words or phrases in the text which the writer uses to give the definitions.

See Vocabulary bank.

---

diabetes mellitus   breast cancer
heart attack   migraine
stomach ulcer   stroke

 **HADFORD** *University*

There are four main essay types in medical studies:

• descriptive
• analytical
• comparison
• argument

(A) What are the advantages and disadvantages of screening for diseases in primary care?

(B) 'Disease prevention is far better than providing cures.' To what extent do you agree with this statement?

(C) Explain why targeting three key behaviours is so important for the developed world.

(D) What aspects of prevention need to be considered by GPs? Describe what is involved in each.

Word/phrase	Meaning
1 screening	test results incorrectly indicating the presence of disease
2 profiling	the management of a condition by the patients themselves, especially common in diabetes
3 lifestyle modification	identifying patients likely to develop specific conditions, using data from patient records
4 self-management	tests for specific conditions carried out on a regular basis
5 false positives	providing advice and encouragement to patients on how to change their behaviour to improve their health

Caring for Our Health
the role of primary care in disease prevention

At the heart of primary care is the concept of preventative medicine, the belief that diseases or disability should be avoided rather than treated. How to put this into practice is something which has to be considered by all general practitioners (GPs). On a purely economic basis, the benefits associated with preventative medicine are considerable. Firstly, resources for treatment are not required. In addition, the individual can continue working and contributing to the economy. Unfortunately, not all conditions can be prevented. Examples include infectious diseases such as salmonella, which can be acquired from contaminated food. However, conditions such as type 2 diabetes can be largely prevented. With a rapidly ageing population in many developing countries, it is important that prevention should have a high priority in primary care.

Three different aspects of prevention need to be taken into account by GPs when considering the services they deliver. Firstly, primary prevention is the promotion of health and the prevention of illness, which involves vaccination programmes and efforts to ensure that a safe environment is provided for individuals. Lifestyle modification (providing advice and encouragement to patients on how to change to healthier behaviours) is a tool to change this at an individual level. Smoking cessation clinics are a good example of this.

At a community level, awareness campaigns can be used to heighten awareness, for example putting up healthy eating posters. Secondary prevention is concerned with the early identification of disease and the provision of prompt treatment to minimize its damage. This can include running screening programmes, where tests for specific conditions are carried out on a regular basis.

Tertiary prevention is about reducing the effects of disease and disability on the patient, which can involve minimizing the patient's suffering using appropriate analgesia (pain relief) or promoting self-management, the management of a condition by the patients themselves. A good example of this is with patients who have diabetes.

GPs can also use screening programmes, in which tests are carried out for a specific condition at regular intervals. Screening can deliver considerable benefits in minimizing the effects of disease. When used with profiling, that is, identifying patients likely to develop specific conditions using data from patient records, it can be very cost effective. Early diagnosis, when conditions or diseases are identified at an early stage, can mean that diseases are easier to treat and can be completely cured in some cases. Diseases screened for include cervical cancer, breast cancer and heart conditions. However, screening is not suitable for all diseases. Some tests can have high levels of false positives – results falsely indicating the presence of disease. Further testing may be required for confirmation, which can be upsetting for patients. Tests can also be expensive and may return few results if incidence rates for a disease are low. Care needs to be taken in deciding whether to set up a screening programme for a specific disease.

In the developed world, targeting three disease-linked behaviours could provide huge benefits in human and financial terms. The first of these is tobacco smoking, causing death through lung cancer and vascular disease as well as chronic obstructive pulmonary diseases. It is estimated that around 100 million deaths were directly attributable to tobacco smoking in the 20th century and that by 2030 this will increase by another billion. Eating too many fatty and sugary foods and not exercising is one of the main causes of diabetes. According to the WHO, diabetes is likely to be one of the most substantial threats to human health in the 21st century, with a projected financial cost of $192 billion by 2020 for the United States alone. If diagnosed early, it can be managed relatively easily. The final behaviour is a reduction in alcohol abuse. Studies show that the misuse of alcohol can be responsible for up to 5% of hospital admissions and can impact significantly on heart disease, diabetes and liver failure. The medical profession has been aware for a long time that population health is improved by prevention. With a rapidly ageing population, it is important that a similar conclusion is reached by governments in the developed world.

A Find the words in the box in the text in Lesson 8.2.

   1 What part of speech is each word?

   2 Think of another word which could be used in place of the word in the text. Use your dictionary if necessary.

> concept   associated   required
> modification   prompt   minimize
> intervals   data   suitable
> upsetting   substantial

B Study sentences A–D.

   1 Identify the dependent clause.

   2 Copy the table under the sentences and write the parts of each dependent clause in the table.

   3 Rewrite the sentence using an active construction.

   Example:

   A *GPs have to consider two key aspects.*

[A] There are two key aspects which have to be considered by GPs.

[B] Care needs to be taken by general practitioners when deciding on a screening programme.

[C] There are many diseases which are caused by three harmful behaviours.

[D] Governments have yet to realize that prevention needs to be prioritized by them.

C Read the essay plans and extracts on the opposite page.

   1 Match each plan with an essay title in Lesson 8.2.

   2 Which essay is each extract from?

   3 Which part of the plan is each extract from?

Subject	Verb	By whom/what
(aspects) which	have to be considered	by all GPs

D Work with a partner.

   1 Write another paragraph for one of the plans.

   2 Exchange paragraphs with another pair. Can they identify where it comes from?

A Make complete sentences from these notes. Add words as necessary.

[A] there – reasons – why – screening – not – effective – all – diseases

[B] conclusion – care – needs – taken – deciding – diseases – screen for

[C] identifying – disease – early stage – easier – treat/cure

[D] screening – carrying – tests – for a – condition – intervals

[E] examples – screening – useful – cervical/breast cancer – heart

[F] screening – delivers – benefits – minimizing – effects – disease

B The sentences in Exercise A are topic sentences for paragraphs in essay A in Lesson 8.2. Put them in the best order for the essay. What is the main topic for each paragraph?

C Look at the essay question on the right.

   1 What kind of essay is this?

   2 Do some research and make an essay plan.

   3 Write the essay.

   See Skills bank.

Dr Brown and his colleagues have a medium-sized urban practice. They have a screening programme for cancer, which has had good results in identifying the disease at an early stage. They are now considering expanding the screening programme to cover Alzheimer's disease. Your task is to produce a paper setting out the advantages and disadvantages of this development and recommending whether or not it should be introduced.

Essay plans

A

1. introduction: importance of screening: essay aims
2. define screening
3. advantages: early diagnosis means easier to treat, possible complete cure
4. examples: cervical/breast cancer, heart conditions
5. disadvantages: false positives, expensive
6. conclusion: care taken in selecting/setting up programme for disease

B

1. introduction: give essay aims
2. definition of prevention
3. three different types of prevention: primary, secondary, tertiary
4. primary: health promotion and illness prevention – anti-smoking clinics
5. secondary: identification of disease and damage limitation – screening for cancer
6. tertiary: minimizing effects of existing disease – diabetes self-management

Essay extracts

1

In medicine, prevention is the belief that diseases or disability should be avoided rather than treated. It can provide very significant benefits by helping to avoid the human and financial costs associated with disease. In this essay, I will look at the three different aspects of prevention which GPs can use when considering their service provision and the benefits that these can deliver in practice.

2

There are reasons why screening is not effective for all diseases. For example, some diseases have a very low incidence, which means that a lot of testing would need to be carried out to identify one case of that disease. Such testing would be time-consuming and costly and would not be cost-effective. Another factor to consider is how well the tests can identify the disease. Some tests can provide false positives, indicating that a patient has a disease when in fact they do not. Further testing is then required to provide a final result and the uncertainty can be very stressful for the patient.

Understanding new words: using definitions

You will often find new words in academic texts. Sometimes you will not be able to understand the text unless you look the word up in a dictionary, but often a technical term will be defined or explained immediately or later in the text.

Look for these indicators:

is or *are*	*Tertiary prevention is about reducing the effects of disease and disability on the patient.*
brackets	*... lifestyle modification (providing advice and encouragement to patients on how to change to healthier behaviours).*
or	*At the heart of primary care is the concept of preventative medicine, the belief that diseases or disability should be avoided rather than treated.*
which	*... primary prevention, which involves vaccination programmes.*
a comma or a dash (–) immediately after the word or phrase	*Early diagnosis, when conditions or diseases are identified at an early stage ...* *Inoculation – vaccinating patients against disease ...*
phrases such as *that is, in other words*	*... profiling: that is, identifying patients likely to develop specific conditions using data from patient records.* *In other words, using patient records to identify those most at risk.*

Remember!

When you write assignments, you may want to define words yourself. Learn to use the methods above to give variety to your written work.

Understanding direction verbs in essay titles

Special verbs called **direction verbs** are used in essay titles. Each direction verb indicates a type of essay. You must understand the meaning of these words so you can choose the correct writing plan.

Kind of essay	Direction verbs
Descriptive	*State ... Say ... Outline ... Describe ... Summarize ... What is/are ...?*
Analytical	*Analyze ... Explain ... Comment on ... Examine ... Give reasons for ... Why ...? How ...?*
Comparison/ evaluation	*Compare (and contrast) ... Distinguish between ... Evaluate ... What are the advantages and/or disadvantages of ...?*
Argument	*Discuss ... Consider ... (Critically) evaluate ... To what extent ...? How far ...?*

Choosing the correct writing plan

When you are given a written assignment, you must decide on the best writing plan before you begin to write the outline. Use key words in the essay title to help you choose – see *Vocabulary bank*.

Type of essay – content	Possible structure
Descriptive writing List **the most important points** of something: e.g., in a narrative, a list of key events in chronological order; a description of key ideas in a theory or from an article you have read. Summarize points in a logical order. **Example:** *Describe the different aspects of prevention to be considered in primary care.*	• **introduction** • **point/event 1** • **point/event 2** • **point/event 3** • **conclusion**

Analytical writing
List the **important points** which **in your opinion** explain the situation.
Justify your opinion in each case.
Look behind the facts at the **how** and **why**, not just **what/who/when**.
Look for and question accepted ideas and assumptions.
Example:
Explain the importance for the developed world of targeting three specific behaviours.
	• **introduction**
	• **definitions**
	• **most important point:**
	  example/evidence/reason 1
	  example/evidence/reason 2, etc.
	• **next point:**
	  example/evidence/reason 3
	  example/evidence/reason 4, etc.
	• **conclusion**

Comparison/evaluation Decide on and define the **aspects** to compare two subjects. You may use these aspects as the basis for paragraphing. Evaluate which aspect(s) is/are better or preferable and give reasons/criteria for your judgment. **Example:** *Compare the relative benefits of primary and secondary prevention.*	• **introduction** • **state and define aspects** **Either:** • **aspect 1:** subject A v. B • **aspect 2:** subject A v. B **Or:** • **subject A:** aspect 1, 2, etc. • **subject B:** aspect 1, 2, etc. • **conclusion/evaluation**
Argument writing **Analyze** and/or **evaluate**, then give your **opinion** in a **thesis statement** at the beginning or the end. Show awareness of difficulties and disagreements by mentioning counter-arguments. **Support** your opinion with evidence. **Example:** *'Screening can provide benefits, regardless of which disease is screened for.' Discuss with examples.*	• **introduction: statement of issue** • **thesis statement giving opinion** • **define terms** • **point 1:** explain + evidence • **point 2:** explain + evidence, etc. •**conclusion:** implications, etc. *Alternatively:* • **introduction: statement of issue** • **define terms** • **for:** point 1, 2, etc. • **against:** point 1, 2, etc. • **conclusion: statement of opinion**

fixed phrases • medical terms

A Match the words to make fixed phrases.

1 barrier   contraceptive
2 family   hazard
3 health   injury
4 health   planning
5 occupational   related
6 population-   risk
7 work-   wide

1	2
to	... start with
the	... people think
	on ... other hand
some	to ... extent
	on ... one hand
many	... real question is
this	on ... grounds that
	... would be great, except
that	in ... sort of situation

HADFORD *University*

? Vaccination
Population-wide vaccination programmes resulted in the eradication of smallpox, as well as the control of infectious diseases such as measles and diphtheria.

• Safer workplaces
Work-related health problems, severe injuries and deaths have been significantly reduced in recent years, fatal occupational injuries around 40% since 1980.

• Family planning
Access to family planning services has resulted in increased opportunities for preconception and counselling; and fewer infant, child and maternal deaths. Barrier contraceptives have helped prevent pregnancy and transmission of HIV.

• Tobacco use as a health hazard
Recognition of tobacco use as a health hazard has changed the promotion of use. Since then, smoking prevalence has decreased, and millions of smoking-related deaths have been prevented.

B Study the words and phrases in the blue box.

1 Complete each phrase in column 2 with a word from column 1.

2 Which phrase can you use to:
  • agree only partly with a point
  • begin talking about several points
  • compare two ideas
  • focus on an important point
  • give a reason for a point
  • mention an idea
  • mention a problem with someone's idea
  • talk about certain circumstances

C Look at the pictures on the opposite page.

1 How can advances in these areas improve public health?

2 Match each picture with the correct text (A–F).

3 Look at the texts A–F. Replace the words in italics with a phrase from Exercise B.

D Read the extract from the Hadford University handout about public health in the US on this page.

1 Match the blue words in this extract with the definitions on the opposite page.

2 Use your dictionary to check words you do not know.

E Complete the table on the right.

See Vocabulary bank.

Base form	Other related forms
control	controlling, controlled
eliminate	
eradicate	
fatal	
infect	
prevent	
transmit	

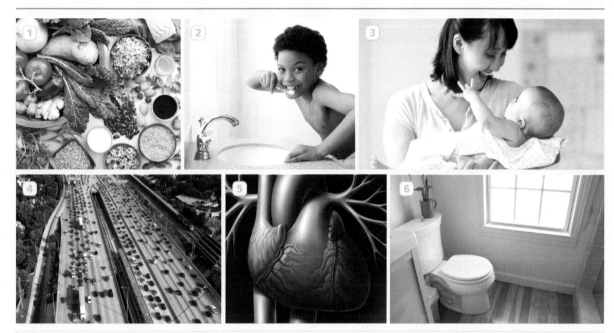

A Control of infectious diseases

Firstly, the control of infectious diseases has been the result of cleaner water and improved sanitation. In addition, there have been public health efforts to control infections such as tuberculosis and sexually transmitted infections (STIs).

B Healthier mothers and babies

Healthier mothers and babies are a result of better hygiene and nutrition, the availability of antibiotics, greater access to health care, and technological advances in maternal and neonatal medicine. *When this happens*, mortality rates drop significantly. Since 1900, infant mortality has decreased by 90% and maternal mortality by 99%.

C Decline in deaths from coronary heart disease and stroke

There has been a decline in deaths from coronary heart disease and strokes *because* risks such smoking have been tackled, and access to early detection and better treatment has been improved.

D Fluoridation of drinking water

Fluoridation of drinking water in the US began in 1945. On the one hand, fluoridation has played an important role in the reduction in tooth decay (40% to 70% in children) as well as in tooth loss in adults (40% to 60%). *However*, some argue that we should have the right to choose whether our water is fluoridated or not.

E Safer and healthier foods

Improvements in food production began in 1900 in the United States. Scientists identified essential micronutrients, and food-fortification programmes were established. These were successful *to a point*, eliminating major nutritional deficiency diseases including rickets, goitre and pellagra.

F Motor vehicle safety

Improvements in motor vehicle safety have contributed to large reductions in motor vehicle-related deaths. These include successful efforts to change personal behaviour (e.g., increased personal safety, as well as decreased drinking and driving incidents).

Definitions

A connected with work

B the fact of being common

C attempting to make something acceptable to people

D controlling the number of children, using birth control

E disease that can be passed on (through the air we breath) to another person

F before conception

G devices that stop someone from becoming pregnant or catching sexually transmitted infections

H passing something on from one person to another

I a danger or a risk to a person's health

J destroyed completely

K related to the whole of the population

L to stop something happening/someone doing something

A Study the slide on the right. What questions do you think the lecturer will answer?

B Listen to Part 1 of the lecture.

1 Complete the *Notes* section below.

2 What is the lecturer's story about? Why is it not given in the notes?

3 Complete the *Summary* section.

4 Answer the *Review* questions.

C Create a blank Cornell diagram. Listen to Part 2 of the lecture.

1 Complete the *Notes* section.

2 Write some *Review* questions.

3 Complete the *Summary* section.

4 Were your questions in Exercise A answered?

D Study the phrases in column 1 of the blue box. Listen to some sentences from the lecture. Which type of information in column 2 follows each phrase?

Public Health (Lecture 1)

- Obesity – extent of problem
- Obesity – solutions
- Climate change – direct & indirect effects

1	2
1 As we shall see, …	a developing trend
2 In terms of …	information about a point the speaker will make later
3 It could be argued that …	an aspect of a topic the speaker wants to focus on
4 Research has shown that …	
5 Increasingly we find that …	a statement the speaker agrees with
6 It's true to say that …	
7 From the point of view of …	a conclusion
8 So it should be clear that …	an idea the speaker may not agree with

Review	Notes
Obesity - definition	Body mass _____ = kg/height m²
	overweight (BMI _____) vs. obesity (BMI _____)
	measure childhood obesity = _____
How big is the problem?	_____ of the problem
	WHO stats for 2015 = _____ obese
	previously high-income countries, now _____ + _____
	income countries
What is the source of the problem?	Causes =
	energy _____ foods ↑/↓ _____ foodstuffs
	↓ phys activity
	↑ use modes of _____
	→ to urban areas from countryside
What are the risks?	Health risks for obese
	obesity + related diseases are l_____ pr_____
	risks = _____ / _____ / _____
	risks for obese children: _____ / _____
Solutions are …?	Increase responsibility of:
	food _____ / m_____ing / legislation
Summary	

See *Skills bank.*

9.3 Extending skills

recognizing digressions • source references

A Study the words and phrases in box a.

1 Mark the stressed syllables.

2 🎧 Listen and check your answers.

3 Which word or phrase in each group has a different stress pattern?

B Study the phrases in box b.

1 Do you think the phrases show a digression (start or end) or a relevant point? Write **D** or **R**.

2 Look at the **D** phrases. Do they start or end the digression?

C 🎧 Listen to the final part of the lecture from Lesson 9.2.

1 Take notes using the Cornell system. Leave spaces if you miss information.

2 What topic does the lecturer mention that is different from the main subject?

3 Why does the lecturer mention this topic?

4 What is your research task?

5 Compare your notes in pairs. Fill in any blank spaces.

6 Complete the *Review* and *Summary* sections.

See *Skills bank*.

Box a

1 calculate, calorie, medical, overweight, vitamin

2 childhood obesity, heat stroke, physical activity, vector-borne disease

3 breast cancer, family planning, gender gap, health risks

4 actually, generally, usually, fundamentally, crucially

Box b

Now, where was I?

It's the first of these points that I'm going to focus on now.

By the way, …

So to get back to the main topic …

I have a little story to tell you …

If we move on now to …

You don't need to take notes on this …

The point of that story was …

If we turn now to …

When we look at public health issues, we'll find …

D 🎧 What information does the lecturer provide about sources? Listen to the extracts and complete the table below.

	Extract 1	Extract 2	Extract 3	Extract 4
Name of writer				
Title and date of source				
Location				
Type of reference				
Relevant to …?				
Introducing phrase				

E Use your notes to write 75–100 words about the effects of climate change on public health.

F Work in groups. Study the public health issues in box c. Choose one topic you would like to find out more about and then discuss these questions.

1 What kind of information will you need to find?

2 What ideas do you have already?

3 Where can you go to find more information?

Box c

flooding

heatwaves

drought

reduced winter temperatures

psychological effects of any of the above

A   Look at the words in the blue box. Identify their stress patterns.

> emphysema   epidemic   eradication
> legislation   obesity   osteoarthritis
> phenomenon   pollutant   salmonella

B   Work in pairs.

Student A: Think of good ways to take part in a seminar.

Student B: Think of bad ways to take part in a seminar.

C   You are going to hear some students in a seminar. They have been asked to discuss the question: *What is the role of countries such as the US and Britain in resolving the impact of climate change on health in the developing world?*

   1   🎧 Listen to the seminar extracts. Decide whether each contribution is good or poor.

   2   Give reasons for your opinion.

   3   Think of some additional information to add to the good contributions.

D   Work in a group of three or four.

   1   Discuss your information for the topics in Lesson 9.3, Exercise F. Agree on the best definition.

   2   Discuss how best to present this information.

   3   Present a definition and description of your topic to the whole class.

E   Study Figure 1 on this page. What do the pictures show?

F   Study the information in Figure 2 on the opposite page. In pairs or groups, discuss the following:

   1   How is the information presented and who is it aimed at? How do you know?

   2   What other information not given here might be useful for this type of publication?

   3   To what extent is this is an effective means of resolving the problem of childhood obesity? Tell the class about your ideas, saying what they are based on.

See Vocabulary bank.

Figure 1

Why does your child's weight matter?

What is the importance of a healthy weight?

It's a known fact that children are getting heavier, and the news is not good for either their health or general well-being. Not only are overweight children more likely to develop diabetes or other diseases later on in life, but they are also more likely to become obese as adults.

Healthy eating for children

Healthy eating begins at home with families sitting down for regular meals all together. However, calorie counting or offering a restricted diet is not necessarily the best option when educating children. Better instead to limit their intake of sugar-rich drinks and high-calorie snacks. Also, try avoiding 'eating on the run', and don't be tempted to give your child sweets and chocolate for comfort or as a reward.

Healthy eating at home and school

Help your child adopt healthy eating habits right from a young age. Many schools are taking part in the National Healthy Schools Eating Programme, and canteen food must now meet new nutritional standards. Getting children to eat healthier options at home will be consistent with what they eat at school and help towards developing lifelong healthy eating habits.

Health is not the only issue

It's not just a question of their physical health; children who are overweight could also experience:
- bullying
- teasing
- low self-esteem.

So what can you do to help? A child who sees their parents or carers following a healthy, active lifestyle will tend to follow their example. By establishing good habits and routines from the beginning, you will be improving your child's quality of life both now and for the future.

Up and active!

In addition to their sports classes at school, here are some ways your children could achieve an hour a day of physical activity:

With you – walking, cycling or scootering to school, playing football, walking the dog, going on a nature trail, playing Frisbee.

At home – dancing to music.

At the leisure centre – swimming, doing gymnastics, trampolining.

Further information can be found at:

www.eatwell.gov.uk/agesandstages/children
www.parentlineplus.org.uk
www.schoolfoodtrust.org.uk

Figure 2

Recognizing fixed phrases from medical studies (2)

Make sure you understand these phrases from medical studies.

barrier contraceptive
infant mortality

health risk
population-wide

ethnic origin
maternal mortality

heat stroke
public health

family planning
middle-income

heatwave
respiratory disorder

health hazard
occupational injury

work-related
human rights

Recognizing fixed phrases from academic English (2)

Make sure you understand these fixed phrases from general spoken academic English.

As we shall see, …

But the real question is …

From the point of view of …

In a case like this, …

In terms of …

In the sense that …

In this sort of situation, …

That's the reason why …

Increasingly, we find that …

It could be argued that …

It's true to say that …

Many people think …

On the grounds that …

On the one hand, …

Research has shown that …

So it should be clear that …

To some extent …

To start with, …

Using the Cornell note-taking system

There are many ways to take notes from a lecture. One method was developed by Walter Pauk at Cornell University, USA.

The system involves **Five Rs**.

record	Take notes during the lecture.
reduce	After the lecture, turn the notes into one- or two-word questions or 'cues' which will help you remember the key information.
recite	Say the questions and answers aloud.
reflect	Decide on the best way to summarize the key information in the lecture.
review	Look again at the key words and the summary (and do this regularly).

Recognizing digressions

Lecturers sometimes move away from the main point in a lecture to tell a story or an anecdote. This is called a **digression**. You must be able to recognize the start and end of digressions in a lecture.

Sometimes a digression is directly relevant to the content of the lecture, sometimes it has some relevance and sometimes, with a poor lecturer, it may be completely irrelevant. Sometimes the lecturer points out the relevance.

Don't worry if you get lost in a digression. Just leave a space in your notes and ask people afterwards.

Recognizing the start	*That reminds me …*
	I remember once …
	By the way, …
Recognizing the end	*Anyway, where was I?*
	Back to the point.
	So, as I was saying, …

Understanding the relevance	*Of course, the point of that story is …*
	I'm sure you can all see that the story shows …
	Why did I tell that story? Well, …

Asking about digressions	*What was the point of the story about Médicins du Monde?*
	Why did the lecturer start talking about note-taking?
	I didn't get the bit about …

Referring to other people's ideas

We often need to talk about the ideas of other people in a lecture or a tutorial. We normally give the name of the writer and/or the name of the source. We usually introduce the reference with a phrase; we may quote directly, or we may paraphrase an idea.

Name and introducing phrase	*As Benjamin points out …*
	To quote Benjamin …
Where	*in Principles of Public Health Medicine …*
What	*we can think of the provision of public health care as …*

10.1 Vocabulary · 'neutral' and 'marked' words • expressing confidence/tentativeness

A Study the words in box a.

1 Use your dictionary to find out the meanings.

2 What part of speech is each word?

B Read the Hadford University handout.

1 Use your dictionary or another source to check the meanings of the highlighted phrases.

2 Which are the stressed syllables in each phrase? Which two phrases have the same stress pattern?

C Look at the pictures on the opposite page.

1 What aspect of evidence-based medicine do you think each picture might relate to?

2 For each aspect, talk about why you think it might be important in evidence-based medicine. Use the highlighted phrases from Exercise B and words from Exercise A.

D Study the words in box b.

1 Check the meanings, parts of speech and stress patterns.

2 Put the words into the correct box in the table below, as in the example.

Neutral	Marked
rise, increase	rocket, soar
fall, decrease	
big, large	
good	
small	

E Read the press release about Aktiv8+ from a health foods producer.

1 Use a marked word from Exercise D in place of each of the blue (neutral) words.

2 Look at the red phrases. How strong or confident are they?

---

a

blinding   control   data   evidence   intervention   meta-analysis   placebo   randomize   significance   validate

---

 **HADFORD** *University*

Randomized control trials

The randomized control trial (RCT) is the best way of studying the effectiveness of a treatment or intervention. Patients in the trial are randomly assigned to one of two groups: the control group or the treatment group. The control group receives a placebo, a treatment with no active ingredients. It is often simply a pill made of sugar. The treatment group receives the drug or intervention being tested. The two groups are needed to show the difference between the placebo effect (which results from patients' belief in the treatment) and the actual effect of the treatment being trialled.

Good trial design ensures the validity of the trial and uses blinding to minimize the placebo effect. In double-blind trials, neither the patient nor the doctor knows which treatment is active. Systematic reviews are summaries of the results of RCTs for a specific intervention. The review can also include a meta-analysis of the statistical results. This can combine the results of different small RCTs as if they were one large RCT.

---

b

brilliant   collapse   enormous   huge   insignificant   massive   minimal   outstanding   plummet   plunge   rocket   significant   slump   soar   superb   tremendous

---

It is clear that Activ8+ is highly effective in treating hypertension. It is generally accepted that PPI, the active ingredient, reduces hypertension. Patients regularly using Aktiv8+ spread have seen their blood pressure fall. Only a small amount of the active ingredient is used. Evidence from a study of 200 patients shows there may be a large reduction in their risk of developing hypertension. The number of patients suffering from diseases related to raised blood pressure has undoubtedly increased recently. Because Aktiv8+ has achieved such good results, it is fair to say that it could play a big role in saving lives. As a result, sales have risen over the past five months.

See *Vocabulary bank.*

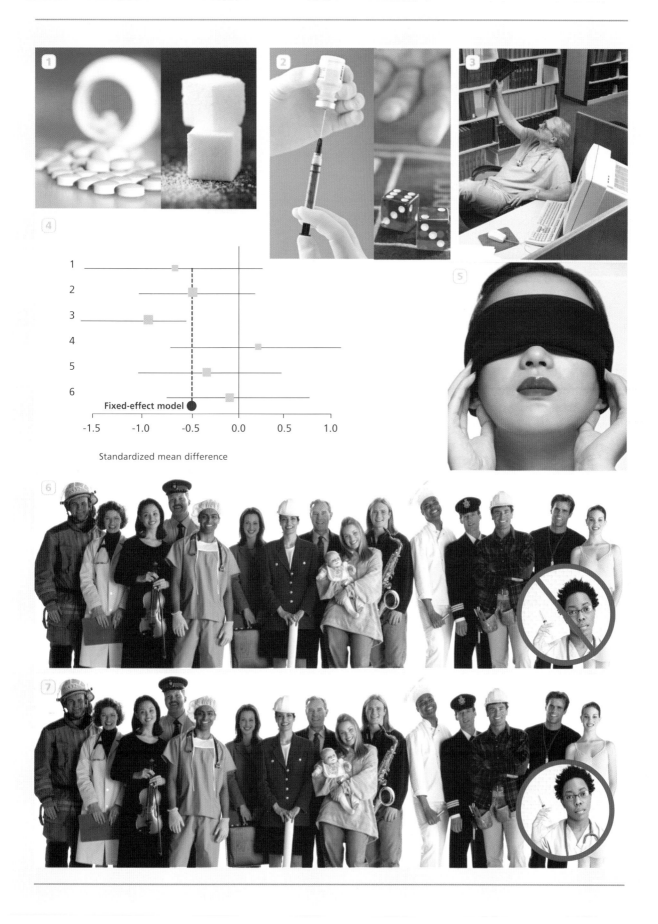

Standardized mean difference

A Study the sentence on the right. Each phrase in box a could go in the space. What effect would each one have on the base meaning? Mark from *** = very confident to * = very tentative.

The use of this intervention _____ an improvement in the condition.

B Survey the text on the opposite page.
1 What will the text be about?
2 Write three research questions.

probably caused _____
may have contributed to _____
was possibly one of the factors which contributed to _____
could have been a factor which led to _____
caused _____
seems to have caused _____

C Read the text. Does it answer your questions?

D Answer these questions.
1 When and where did evidence-based medicine begin?
2 What is the main benefit of evidence-based medicine?
3 Do you think summarizing the best available evidence or getting it to the point of patient care poses the greater problem? Why?
4 Are doctors likely to use all the information they are presented with when deciding on treatments?
5 Can the effectiveness of evidence-based clinical guidelines vary according to who is responsible for finding the evidence?
6 Does it take a long time to make new additions to the online resource Clinical Evidence?

It is generally agreed that ... _____
Most practitioners seem to agree ... _____
The literature suggests ... _____
Evidence from the literature indicates ... _____
It is clear that ... _____
The consensus is ... _____
Some writers have suggested ... _____

E Find the phrases in box b in the text. Is the writer *confident* (**C**) or *tentative* (**T**) about the information which follows?

Example:

The end result | is also | a set of clinical guidelines | but | as these | are tailored to | the specific situation | the evidence suggests | they | are more likely | to be effective. |

F Look at the writer's description of the difficulties faced in implementing of evidence-based medicine in practice (paragraph 2).
1 Underline the marked words.
2 What does the choice of words suggest about the writer's opinion of the difficulties faced?
3 Find neutral words to use in their place.

A

Most practitioners seem to agree that best practice is desirable but the literature suggests that there are enormous barriers to introducing EBM into clinical practice.

G Study the example sentence on the right, and then sentences A and B.
1 Divide sentences A and B into small parts, as in the example sentence.
2 Underline any linking words (e.g., conjunctions).
3 Find the subjects, verbs, objects/complements and adverbial phrases which go together.
4 Make several short simple sentences which show the meaning.

B

The number of research articles has rocketed over the past 20 years and doctors do not have time to identify and read all the available evidence for themselves.

See Skills bank.

Evidence-based medicine in the clinical setting

It is generally agreed that the term *evidence-based medicine* (EBM) emerged in 1991 from the work of a group of doctors at McMaster University, Ontario (Sackett et al., 1997). It outlined three different elements which needed to be combined in order to provide the best level of patient care possible. Firstly, the best available evidence should be used when deciding what treatment the patient should receive. Secondly, the experience of the doctor administering treatment should be fully used when making the decision. Lastly, that the choice of the patient should be taken into consideration. The clinical benefits from using evidence-based medicine for patients are clearly evident, but there are also economic benefits. Sackett (et al., 1996) states that evidence-based medicine is a 'conscientious, explicit and judicious use of current best evidence in making decisions about the care of individual patients.'

Most practitioners seem to agree that best practice is desirable, but the literature suggests that there are enormous barriers to introducing evidence-based medicine into clinical practice. Evidence from the literature indicates that the most important of these barriers is the difficulty of identifying the best treatment for any given condition. The number of research articles has rocketed over the past 20 years, and doctors do not have time to identify and read all the available evidence for themselves. As Greenhalgh (2006) states, 'Only a tiny proportion of medical research breaks entirely new ground.' Clearly, then, not all papers are relevant. It is clear that systematic reviews which gather together and evaluate all the evidence on a clinical topic can help overcome this tremendous problem. The consensus is that systematic reviews which use only randomized control trials are a 'gold standard' of evidence in terms of the effectiveness of treatments. Producing these can be a prolonged process however, with only 5,000 produced by 2007. For this reason, Clinical Evidence (2009) is an outstanding additional resource. It summarizes the significance and implications of new research as it is published, keeping doctors up to date with important changes.

Some writers have suggested that there are two approaches to implementing evidence-based medicine in a hospital. The top-down approach involves management implementing detailed clinical guidelines for all procedures using the best available evidence. By then ensuring that health care staff adhere closely to these guidelines, management can be certain that the work carried out by doctors is in line with best practice. A bottom-up approach is where the clinical staff themselves are encouraged to find the best available evidence for procedures and to evaluate it in relation to their own working situations. The end result is also a set of clinical guidelines, but as these are tailored to the specific situation, the evidence indicates they are more likely to be effective.

As a recent article indicates, getting evidence to the doctor when decisions are being made on treatment choices is the ultimate problem. The authors suggest integrating the evidence into IT systems which are used for decision support. Their evidence suggests that this 'presents an opportunity to both reduce medical errors and improve delivery of evidence-based patient care' (Starmer et al., 2006). However, others have pointed out that doctors can choose to ignore this information if they wish (Glasziou and Haynes, 2005). These writers have claimed that small teams are very efficient at implementing guidelines when they focus on clearly defined problem areas and update their knowledge in an organic way by regularly reviewing their procedures.

A Read the three essay questions. What types of essay are they?

B Look at text A on the opposite page. Copy and complete Table 1.

C Look at text B on the opposite page. Copy and complete Table 2.

D Look again at the solutions in Exercise B (Table 1). What are their possible advantages and disadvantages?

E Read the title of essay 3 again.

1 Make a plan for this essay.

2 Write a topic sentence for each paragraph in the body of the essay.

3 Write a concluding paragraph.

1 Compare the usefulness of the methods an organization might use to introduce an evidence-based medicine approach to treatment.

2 Explain from a practical viewpoint the limitations of systematic reviews in achieving evidence-based medicine goals.

3 Describe, with some actual examples, the difficulties faced by organizations implementing an evidence-based medicine approach. Consider how they can best solve these difficulties.

Table 1

Situation	
Problem	
Solutions	

Table 2

Solution	
Argument for	
Argument against	

A Expand these simple sentences. Add extra information. Use the ideas in Lesson 10.3.

1 Providing timely, high-quality evidence can be difficult.

2 Many staff may not use evidence-based clinical guidelines effectively.

3 Clinicians are more likely to use guidelines they have helped develop.

4 Integrating clinical guidelines into patient support systems has potential.

B Look at text C on the opposite page. Copy and complete Tables 1–3.

Table 1: *Referencing books*

Author(s)	Place	Date	Publisher

C Look at text D on the opposite page.

1 Complete a further row of Table 1.

2 How could you write this as a reference?

Table 2: *Referencing journals*

Name of journal	Volume	Pages

D What do the abbreviations in the blue box mean?

Table 3: *Referencing websites*

Retrieval date	URL

E Look back at the text on page 81 (Lesson 10.2) and at texts A and B on the opposite page.

1 Find all the research sources (e.g., Sackett et al., 1997).

&	©	cf.	edn.	ed(s).	et al.
ibid.	n.d.	op. cit.	p.	pp.	vol.

2 Mark the page numbers for books and journals next to the correct reference in the list (C) on the opposite page.

3 What punctuation and formatting is used before and within each direct quote? Why?

4 What words are used to introduce each direct quote? Why does the writer choose each word?

See *Skills bank.*

A

Case Study 1

An example of an integrated, long-term approach to developing clinical guidelines comes from University Hospital Swendon. They have developed a strategic plan for the revision and full implementation of clinical guidance for all procedures by 2012. Appropriate evidence-based clinical guidelines can be an effective tool for ensuring medical staff are providing the best possible care. (Sackett et al., 1997, p.169).

However, it is important that the guidelines are used effectively in practice. An audit of clinical procedures in the hospital showed that less than 30% of the staff were using them effectively.

The new guidelines will be based on the available evidence, using systematic reviews and material from Clinical Evidence (http://clinicalevidence.bmj.com/ceweb/about/index.jsp). Detailed discussions with relevant staff, following a journal club model, will be used to ensure that the new guidelines are effective in meeting local conditions.

Another important feature of the guidelines is to follow the suggestions put forward by Starmer J et al. (2006, p.753), to integrate them with the new computerized clinical support system which the hospital is currently trialling.

(Source: Cheeseman, 2008)

B

It is clear that the introduction of evidence-based medicine in an organization cannot rely only on the use of cinical guidelines. Glasziou (2005) suggests that a significant proportion of doctors need to be pursuaded to make changes to their practice. If doctors feel that the guidelines are being imposed on them they will be less likely to use them.

However, there can be significant difficulties in involving doctors in creating guidelines (Greenhalgh, 2006:139). Not least among these is the time required. The introduction of guidelines, which can then be modified by doctors, is a useful compromise. By encouraging doctors to take responsibility for the updating of guidelines and matching them to local needs it is more likely that doctors will incorporate new evidence into the guidelines as it is made available.

C

References

Sackett D, Richardson W, Rosenberg W, Haynes R. Evidence-Based Medicine: How to Practice and Teach EBM. New York: Churchill Livingstone; 1997.

Sackett DL, Rosenberg WM, Gray JA, Haynes RB, Richardson WS. Evidence-based medicine: what it is and what it isn't. BMJ. 1996 Jan 3;312(7023): 71–2.

Greenhalgh T. How to Read a Paper: The Basics of Evidence-Based Medicine. 3rd ed. London: Wiley-Blackwell; 2006.

BMJ Publishing. Clinical Evidence: The international source of the best available evidence for effective health care. Retrieved May 26, 2009 from: http://clinicalevidence.bmj.com/ceweb/about/index.jsp

Starmer J, Lorenzi N, Pinson CW. The Vanderbilt EvidenceWeb – developing tools to monitor and improve compliance with evidence-based order sets. AMIA Annu Symp Proc. 2006; 2006:749–753.

Glasziou P, Haynes B. The paths from research to improved health outcomes. ACP J. Club. 2005 Apr;142(2):8–10.

D

Approaches to evidence-based medicine

Dr James Cheeseman

Chatham & Bryant

First published in 2006
by Chatham & Bryant Ltd.
22 Tolley Street, London WC1 6RE
© 2006 James Cheeseman
Reprinted 2008

British Library Cataloguing-in-Publication Data
A catalogue record for this book is available from the British Library

Typeset by Quickset Graphics, Madeley Lane, Slough
Printed and bound by EMTI Ltd, Maidstone, Kent
ISBN 0898159281

Recognizing fixed phrases from medicine (3)

Make sure you understand these key phrases from evidence-based medicine.

active ingredients
blinding
control group
double-blind
evidence

intervention
meta-analysis
placebo effect
randomized control trial
randomly assigned

significance
systematic reviews
treatment group
trial design
validate

Recognizing fixed phrases from academic English (3)

Make sure you understand these key phrases from general academic English.

One of the ...
In some circumstances, ...
The data suggests/indicates ...
... , as follows: ...
The writers assert/maintain that ...

In this sort of situation, ...
It is obvious/clear that ...
It appears to be the case that ...
Research has shown ...
The evidence does not support this idea.

Recognizing levels of confidence in research or information

In an academic context, writers will usually indicate the level of confidence in information they are giving. When you read a 'fact' in a text, look for qualifying words before which show the level of confidence.

Examples:

It appears to be the case that ... / This suggests that ... **(tentative)**
The evidence shows that ... / It is clear that ... **(definite/confident)**

Recognizing 'marked' words

Many common words in English are 'neutral', i.e., they do not imply any view on the part of the writer or speaker. However, there are often apparent synonyms which are 'marked'. They show attitude, or stance.

Examples:

Cases of influenza **rose** by 10% last year. **(neutral)**
Cases of influenza **soared** by 10% last year. **(marked)**

Soared implies that the writer thinks this is a particularly big or fast increase.

When you read a sentence, think: Is this a neutral word, or is it a marked word? If it is marked, what does this tell me about the writer's attitude to the information?

When you write a sentence, particularly in paraphrasing, think: Have I used neutral words or marked words? Do the words show my real attitude/the attitude of the original writer?

Extend your vocabulary by learning marked words and their exact effect.

Examples:

Neutral	marked
go up, rise, increase	soar, rocket
go down, fall, decrease	sink, plummet, plunge
say, state	assert, maintain, claim, argue, allege
big, large	enormous, huge, massive
small	insignificant, minimal

Identifying the parts of a long sentence

Long sentences contain many separate parts. You must be able to recognize these parts to understand the sentence as a whole. Mark up a long sentence as follows:

- Locate the subjects, verbs and objects/complements and underline the relevant nouns, verbs and adjectives.
- Put a dividing line:
  - at the end of a phrase which begins a sentence
  - before a phrase at the end of the sentence
  - between clauses
- Put brackets round extra pieces of information.

Examples:

These <u>writers</u> <u>have</u> <u>claimed</u> | that small <u>teams</u> <u>are</u> very <u>efficient</u> (at implementing guidelines) | when <u>they</u> <u>focus</u> <u>on</u> clearly defined problem <u>areas</u> | and <u>update</u> their <u>knowledge</u> in an organic way (by regularly reviewing their procedures).

Constructing a long sentence

Begin with a very simple SV(O)(C)(A) sentence and then add extra information.

Example:

		reviews	summarize		findings	
As we have seen,	systematic			numerous research		so that clinicians can quickly evaluate their importance.

Writing a bibliography/reference list

The Vancouver system of referencing is commonly used in medicine. Information should be given as shown in the following source references for a book, an Internet article and a journal article. The final list should be in the order in which the references appear in the essay. See the reference list on page 83 for a model.

Author	Title of book	Place of publication	Publisher	Date
Sackett D, Richardson W, Rosenberg W, Haynes R.	Evidence-based medicine: how to practice and teach EBM.	New York	Churchill Livingstone;	1997.

Writer or organization	Title of Internet article	Date of retrieval	Full URL
BMJ Publishing	Clinical evidence	Retrieved Sept 2008	from: http://clinicalevidence.bmj.com/ceweb/about/index.jsp

Author	Title of article	Title of journal	Date	Volume and issue numbers	page numbers
Sackett DL, Rosenberg WM, Gray JA, Haynes RB, Richardson WS.	Evidence-based medicine: what it is and what it isn't.	BMJ.	1996 Jan 3;	312(7023):	71–2.

More information on referencing can be found at
http://www.nlm.nih.gov/bsd/uniform_requirements.html
http://www.bma.org.uk/library_medline/electronic_resources/factsheets/LIBReferenceStyles.jsp#Vancouver

11.1 Vocabulary · linking ideas

A Look at the diagram on the opposite page.

1 Find and mark:
- the ethical principles *(E)*
- the responsibilities of doctors *(R)*
- the examples *(e.g.)*

2 Think of other examples for each principle.

B Study the linking words and phrases in box a.

1 Put them into two groups for:

a discussing reasons and results

b building an argument

2 Is each linking word used to join ideas:

a within a sentence?

b between sentences?

3 Can you think of similar linking words?

4 Put the linking words in 1b in a suitable order to list points in support of an argument.

C Study the words in box b.

1 Are the words nouns, verbs, adjectives or adverbs?

2 What is their stress pattern?

3 What other words or phrases have the same meaning?

D 🎧 Read the text on the right.

1 Complete each space with a word or phrase from box a or box b. Change the form if necessary. Listen and check.

2 Can you think of other words or phrases with the same meaning as the words in blue?

3 Find all the words and phrases in the text connected with *doctor* and *patient*.

E Answer the general knowledge questions on the opposite page.

See Vocabulary bank.

---

a finally   as a result   because   firstly   for example   moreover   one result is that   secondly   so

b conflicting   consent   dignity   dilemma   ethical   explicit   implicit   justice   justify   negligence   principle   respect   responsibility   underlying   uniformly

---

According to Beauchamp and Childers (2001), an _____ approach to medicine requires doctors to _____ the principles of autonomy, beneficence, non-malfeasance and _____. These are _____ in most clinical guidelines, but there is a strong case for making them _____.

_____, it could help in decision-making in the clinical setting. _____, a patient who is a Seventh Day Adventist may refuse to _____ to treatment, such as a life-saving blood transfusion, on religious grounds. This is difficult for a medical practitioner _____ respecting the _____ of autonomy means giving a person undergoing treatment the right to make decisions about their care. However, respecting the principle of beneficence obliges them to cure the sick person if possible. _____ of these _____ requirements, physicians can face an ethical _____. If local clinical guidelines explicitly state the ethical principles, doctors can be sure their decisions are ethically sound. _____, the caregiver can clearly explain the ethical grounds for decisions, which helps the doctor to preserve the patient's _____. _____, if the principle of justice is applied in the guidelines, doctors find it easier to _____ their choice of treatment to patients. For example, national guidelines on recommended drugs are not always applied _____. _____ patients may not get the most effective one for their condition and _____ are likely to complain. If the ethical reasons for the choice are made clear, the doctor can explain these to the patient. _____, by clarifying the _____ ethical principles, those called upon to apply them can see inconsistencies much more easily.

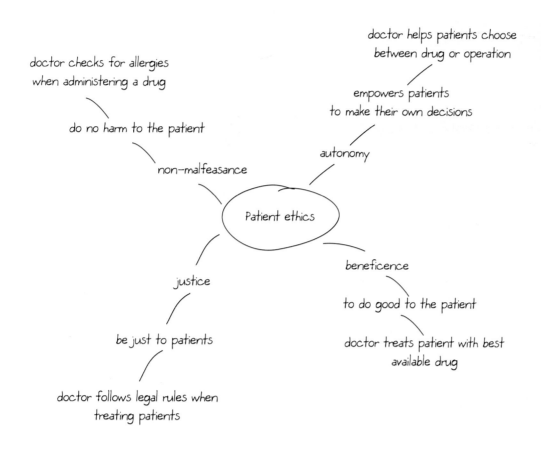

General knowledge quiz

Who or what are these?

   a The Declaration of Helsinki

   b The Doctors' Trial at Nuremberg

   c The European Medicines Agency

   d The Food and Drug Administration

   e The National Institute for Clinical Excellence

   f The Tuskegee Study

Which ethical principle do you think they may relate to?

A You are going to listen to a lecture by a guest speaker in the Medical Studies Department at Hadford University. Look at the poster on the right.

  1 What is the lecture going to be about?

  2 Decide on how you are going to make notes. Prepare a page in your notebook.

B 🎧 Listen to Part 1 of the lecture and make notes.

  1 What is the lecturer's area of expertise?

  2 What are the two main issues that the lecturer will discuss?

  3 What examples does he give?

  4 What ethical principles from Lesson 11.1 do the examples relate to?

C 🎧 Listen to Part 2 of the lecture and make notes.

D Using your notes, answer the questions on the handout on the right.

E Refer to the model Cornell notes on page 107.

  1 Check your answers with the model.

  2 Complete the *Review* and *Summary* sections of the Cornell notes.

F 🎧 The lecturer talks about the consent form. Listen again to part of the lecture. What words tell us whether the information is fact or opinion?

G 🎧 Study the phrases in the blue box. Which type of information below follows each phrase? Listen to some sentences from the lecture.

  • restatement
  • definite point
  • summary of a source
  • example
  • statement of a topic
  • another point
  • tentative point
  • clarification
  • purpose for speaking

H Write out one section of your notes in complete sentences.
  See Skills bank.

 **HADFORD** *University*

Visiting Speaker: Dr Balbir Singh
20th March 5.00 p.m.

'Informed or not, the ethics of consent?'

Dr Singh will explore key ethical principles influencing doctors' interaction with their patients.

---

1 What topic did the lecture cover first?

2 What assumption does the lecturer contradict?

3 What was the importance of the Nuremberg Code, according to the lecturer?

4 What was at the centre of the code?

5 What was the consequence of the Declaration of Helsinki for doctors?

6 What is the lecturer's attitude to the belief by some doctors that patients do not have enough medical knowledge and expertise to properly evaluate the risks and benefits of a procedure?

7 What example of a specific barrier to informed patient consent does he discuss?

8 What does he conclude from the research?

9 What is the most important consideration the lecturer suggests needs to be taken into account when gaining patient consent?

---

1 that is to say

2 Don't misunderstand me.

3 To some degree, ...

4 it's fair to say that ...

5 Not only that, but ...

6 in an attempt to ...

7 to the extent that ...

8 A case in point ...

9 ... gives a (very) good description of ... in ...

10 With respect to ...

11 Briefly, (she) explains how ...

12 (She) has no doubt that ...

11.3 Extending skills

stress in phrases • building an argument

A Study the phrases in box a.

1 Mark the stressed syllables in each phrase.

2 🎧 Listen and check your answers.

3 Which phrases have adjective + noun? Which word has the stronger stress in these phrases?

B Look at the topics below.

- regulatory aspects of biomedical research
- examples of the failure of biomedical research ethics

1 What would you like to know about these topics?

2 Prepare a page in your notebook to make some notes.

3 🎧 Listen to the final part of the lecture (Part 3) and make notes. If there is information which you miss, leave a space.

4 Compare your notes with someone else. Fill in any blank spaces.

C Answer the questions on the Hadford University handout, using your notes.

D Study the stages of building an argument (a–f) in box b.

1 Put the stages in an appropriate order.

2 Match each stage (a–f) with a phrase from box c.

E Look at box b again.

1 🎧 Listen to a section from the lecture. Make notes on what the lecturer says for each stage of the argument (a–f).

2 Check your answers to Exercises D and E1.

F Use your notes to write 75–100 words about the main points in the final part of the lecture.

G In groups, discuss the research task set by the lecturer. Talk about these questions:

1 What are the two contexts you need to consider?

2 Which one will you choose?

3 What ideas do you already have?

4 What kind of information will you need to find?

5 Where can you go and find more information?

6 Report back to the class on your discussion. In Lesson 11.4, you will take part in a seminar on this topic.

Box a

biomedical research
informed consent
research subject
legal regulation
moral rights
the degree of risk
research protocols
research governance

HADFORD *University*

1 What is research governance?

2 Why is the storage of research data particularly important for patients?

3 What does the lecturer say is happening because of increased regulation of drug testing?

4 What does the lecturer think the Tuskegee Study is a good example of?

5 Why is the study still causing debate?

6 What is your research task?

Box b

a giving a counter argument
b giving your opinion
c stating the issue
d supporting the reason with evidence
e rejecting a counter argument
f giving a reason for your opinion

Box c

It's quite clear that …
The question is …
The research has concluded that …
I'm afraid that just isn't true.
Some people claim …
The evidence lies in the fact that …

A Study the terms in box a.

  1 Explain the meaning of the terms.

  2 Mark the main stress in each term.

B Study the words in box b. Match the words in columns 1 and 2 to make phrases.

C Study the Hadmore Research Ethics Committee web page on the opposite page.

  1 From the pictures, identify four factors to be considered in an application for research approval.

  2 What can be used to show that patient consent and safety have been considered in the application?

  3 What can help to show the benefits of the research when making an application?

D Study the phrases in box c.

  1 What purpose would you use these phrases for in a seminar?

  2 Which phrases can you use for linking your new point to a contribution by another speaker?

E 🎧 Listen to some students taking part in a seminar. They have been asked to discuss ethical issues in relation to treatment and research. While you listen, make a note of:

  1 the main topic of each extract

  2 further details of each topic

F Study the Patient Protection Authority web page and discuss these questions.

  1 What is the main message from this page?

  2 What are the three ways in which patient data can be released?

  3 What examples are there of situations in which patient data can be accidentally released?

  4 Think of an example of where it might be necessary to release data in the public interest.

G Discuss your research findings on examples of ethical conflicts in treatment and research with your group. One person from the group should report the conclusions of the discussion to the class.

---

a

Human Tissue Act
patient identifiable information
patient information sheet
statistical data sets
target patient group

---

b

1	2
clinical	benefits
data	interest
health	justification
multi-centre	status
preclinical	testing
proposed	trial
public	outcome
societal	protection
trial	study

---

c

I'd like to start by explaining …

To carry on from this point, I want secondly to look at …

I don't think that is the main reason.

That seems like a very good point X is making.

I'm going to expand the topic by mentioning …

On the other hand, you might want to say that …

As well as this issue, we can also look at a very different issue.

So to sum up, we can say that …

Does anybody have any opinions or anything they would like to add?

I think we need a different viewpoint.

OK, to continue then, …

Following on from what X has said, …

A

HADMORE RESEARCH ETHICS COMMITTEE

Resources and Guidance

These pages contain resources to help applicants produce good quality applications for clinical trials.
To ensure a successful application, it is essential that these examples are followed carefully.

Extracts from successful applications

Clinical justification for proposed trial

Implications of outcome of trial for target patient group

Societal benefits of outcome of trial

Economic justifications for trial

Statement of conflict of interest

Legal guidance

Guidelines on confidentiality compliance within Data Protection Act (1998)

Guidelines on compliance with Human Tissue Act (2004)

Useful research papers

Jones AM, Bamford B. The other face of research governance. BMJ. 2004 Jul 31;329(7460):280–281

Elwyn G, Seagrove A, Thorne K, Cheung WY. Ethics and research governance in a multi-centre study. BMJ. 2005 Apr 9;330(7495):847

Patient consent and safety

Sample patient information sheets

Sample consent forms

Sample current health status checklist

Sample checklist for pre-clinical testing

B

Patient Protection Authority

Home	Defining patient identifiable information	Releasing data with patient's consent	Releasing data in public interest	Preventing accidental disclosure	Meeting Data Protection Act requirements

Preventing accidental disclosure

Legally and ethically, patients have a right for any information provided during treatment or research to be kept confidential and used only for the purpose for which it was provided. This section looks at how the disclosure of Patient Identifiable Information (PII) can be prevented. Click the headings below for more information on each topic.

Transferring data (to other departments, institutions or organizations)

Disposal of personal data

Creating statistical data sets from patient data

Ensuring security of electronic records system

Managing access to electronic records system

Linking words

We use linking words and phrases to join ideas together in a sequence, to show how the ideas are related.

Some linking words can be used to join independent and dependent clauses in a sentence.

Examples:

Carrying out clinical trials has become more difficult **because** the regulation of research in the UK has increased. OR **Because** the regulation of research in the UK has increased, carrying out clinical trials has become more difficult.

Other linking words join sentences in a text.

Example:

Regulation in the UK regarding clinical trials has increased. **As a result**, carrying out research has become more difficult.

When building an argument, it is a good idea to use linking words to add points.

Examples:

Firstly, …	Another point is …	In addition, …	… whereas …
For example, …	Secondly, …	Moreover, …	Finally, …

Using words with similar meanings to refer back in a text

It is a good idea to learn several words with similar or related meanings. We often build cohesion in a text by using different words to refer back to something previously mentioned.

Examples:

First mention	Second mention	Third mention
doctor	medical practitioner	physician
patient	person undergoing treatment	sick person

Recognizing fixed phrases from academic English (4)

In Units 7, 9 and 10 we learnt some key fixed phrases from general academic English. Here are some more to use when speaking.

Don't misunderstand me.	the history of …
I'm afraid that just isn't true.	the presence of …
in an attempt to …	there is a correlation between … and …
… is a case in point.	to some degree …
not only that, but …	to the extent that …
Some people say …	What's more, …
the effect of …	with respect to …

Writing out notes in full

When making notes, we use as few words as possible. This means that when we come to write up the notes, we need to pay attention to:

- the use of numbers, letters and symbols for words and ideas, e.g.,
  Notes: (a) (unable to give consent, e.g., drink/drugs/mental illness)
  One example of a patient unable to give consent is someone under the influence of drugs.

- making sure the grammatical words are put back in, e.g.,
  Notes: →'Gillick standard' (mature enough to give consent)
  The 'Gillick Standard' is whereby minors are considered mature enough to give consent, despite their age.

- making the implied meanings clear, e.g.,
  Notes: None (acc. speaker)
  According to the speaker, there are no examples.

Building an argument

A common way to build an argument is:

1 First, state the issue:
  The question is then: Is this legal regulation justified?

2 Next, give a counter argument:
  There are those who claim that imposing this regulation on research simply increases the time needed to bring drugs onto the market, which may cost people their lives.

3 Then give your opinion:
  I'm afraid that just isn't true.

4 Then give evidence for your opinion:
  The research has concluded that regulatory regimes do a great deal to protect patients from unsafe and ineffective drugs and help safeguard the health of the volunteers who test them.

Linking to a previous point when your contribution is new

When you want to move the discussion in a new direction, introduce your comments with phrases such as:
Following on from what X said, I'd like to talk about …
I'm going to expand the topic by mentioning …
As well as (ethical issues), we can also look at a very different sort of issue.

Summarizing a source

When we talk about the ideas of other people in a lecture or a seminar, we often give a summary of the source in a sentence or two.

Examples:
A book by (name of writer) *called* (name of book) *published in* (year) *gives an explanation of how …*

Briefly, (name of writer) *explains how …*

An introduction to (topic) *can be found in* (name of writer).

A Study the words in box a.

1 What part of speech is each word?

2 Which nouns can be changed to verbs? Which verbs can be changed to nouns? Check the stress and pronunciation.

3 What do the underlined prefixes mean?

a

chromosome   correlate
customize   <u>dys</u>function
encode   gene   <u>geno</u>mics
heredity   molecular   mutation
<u>nano</u>technology   <u>pan</u>demic
<u>patho</u>gen   patent
pharma<u>co</u>genomics   sequencing
stigma   variation

B Study the words in box b. Match each word in the left-hand column with a word in the right-hand column.

Example: *base pair*

b

base	cell
clinical	pair
human	goal
key	trials
societal	findings
stem	genome
ultimate	issues

C Read the headings of each text on the opposite page.

1 What theme links the four texts together?

2 Read text A and look at the highlighted words. Connect each word to the noun it refers to.

Example: *those* refers to previously mentioned nouns (*organs* and *tissues*)

D Study the verbs in box c. They can be used to introduce quotations or paraphrases/summaries.

1 Check the meanings of any words you don't know.

2 Which verbs have similar meanings?

3 Which verbs are not followed by *that*?

4 When can you use each verb?

Example: *accept* = the writer (reluctantly) thinks this idea from someone else is true

c

accept	agree
argue	assert
cite	claim
concede	consider
contend	describe
disagree	dispute
emphasize	illustrate
indicate	insist
note	observe
point out	report
show	state
suggest	

E Read text B on the opposite page. Look at the highlighted sentences.

1 What is the purpose of each sentence?

Example: *A child born in Sweden …* = statement of fact

2 In an assignment, should you refer to the highlighted sentences by **quoting directly** or **paraphrasing**?

3 Choose an appropriate introductory verb and write out each sentence as a direct quotation or a paraphrase. Add the source reference where necessary.

F 1 Read each of the texts again and decide which principles of medical ethics are relevant to the future developments discussed in each.

2 Discuss and write a short summary of your conclusions.

See *Vocabulary bank.*

Schematic of human DNA

A Cloning and regenerative medicine

Currently, organs and tissues from living donors are transplanted in order to replace those which are failing or destroyed. However, in many cases the demand for replacement organs far outstrips supply, to the point where they are for sale, offered by poverty-stricken donors in third-world countries. A new method of organ replacement, using deceased donors, has now been developed. It has been used successfully in an operation to provide a patient with a new trachea. This process replaces the DNA in the donated organ, using stem cells generated from the recipient's tissue. In the case of the trachea transplant it took almost six weeks to complete. Because of the DNA transfer, the recipient's body recognized the transplanted trachea as her own and did not reject it. This is a major development, which holds out the potential of using the technique for other hollow organs, such as lungs, in the near future.

Underton R, Ahmad S. Cloning and regenerative medicine. American Journal of Medical Ethics. 2007 May 31;53(11): 132–9

B A model for ending global inequalities in health

A child born in Sweden is almost 30 times more likely to reach the age of five than a child born in Swaziland. While the national rates conceal variations in mortality between rich and poor, urban and rural, it is possible to suggest that national wealth is the key factor in determining mortality. However, the evidence clearly indicates that mortality is affected by factors other than national wealth. The most striking example is the comparison between the United States and Cuba. Though life expectancy in both is virtually identical, the former spends less than $200 per person on healthcare while the latter spends almost $4,400 per person. Cooper R et al. (2006) state that much of this is due to relatively small amounts invested in infrastructure combined with a well-developed public health strategy. As Cooper R et al. go on to emphasize, 'if the experience of Cuba could be extended to other poor and middle-income countries human health would be transformed'. However, since the 1980s Cuba has also been involved in technology developments. The research, development and marketing of advanced drugs on a worldwide scale illustrates how much can be achieved by a low-income country.

Findless M. A model for ending global inequalities in health. International Journal of Epidemiology. 2006 Jan 31; 25(4):817–824

C The medical potential of nanotechnology

Developments in nanotechnology have enormous potential to revolutionize drug delivery systems. The overall aim is to allow drugs to be delivered to the areas within the body which they are targeting. The active ingredients of drugs are placed inside a wrapper that is genetically designed to locate a particular part of the body. The wrapper is attracted to the cell receptors of the relevant area and attaches to it, discharging its active ingredients. Early results are very impressive. Delivering anti-cancer drugs to the brain has been a major problem due to the blood-brain barrier. However, anti-cancer drugs bound to nanomaterials have successfully crossed the blood-brain barrier and released the drugs at therapeutic concentrations in the brain.

Ratchett C, Brown G, Rail M, Weng F. The medical potential of nanotechnology. Nature Nanotechnology. 2008 Nov 31; 3(11): 635–6

D Dealing with future pandemics

It is not clear where the HIV virus emerged from. What is clear is that since the recognition of the pandemic in 1981, around 25 million people worldwide have lost their lives to it. The anti-retroviral drugs which have helped fight HIV/AIDS owe little to the advances in genetic research which have taken place over the last 15 years. It is to this research that we must look when we face up to new threats of pandemics. The example of H5N1 (also known as bird flu), which appeared to jump from birds to humans, is perhaps the most widely known. The great understanding of human biology and viral reproduction which has emerged from recent research into the human genome gives us a vital weapon in this fight. However, the delay in providing victims of AIDS with the anti-retroviral drugs to fight the disease, because of the desire of the drugs companies to make money, suggests that this knowledge may not be equally applied to all countries and individuals.

Braines G, Kahn M. Dealing with future pandemics. Virology Journal. 2008 Sept 31; 5(1):133-142.

A Discuss the following questions.

1 Why do you think research into the human genome is particularly important for the future of medicine?

2 How do you think such research can help doctors deliver better care to their patients?

B Survey the text on the opposite page. What will the text be about? Write three questions to which you would like answers.

C Read the text. Does it answer your questions?

D Number the sentences on the right 1–8 to show the order in which they happened.

E For each paragraph:

1 Identify the topic sentence.

2 Think of a suitable title.

F Look at the underlined words in the text. What do they refer back to?

G Study the highlighted words and phrases.

1 What do they have in common?

2 What linking words or phrases can you use to show:

   • contrast?
   • concession?
   • reason?
   • result?

3 Write the sentences with the highlighted items again, using other linking words or phrases with similar meanings.

H Read the text on the right. A student has written about some of the technical issues associated with the Human Genome Project, but the quotations and paraphrases have not been correctly done. Can you spot the mistakes and correct them?

I Write a paragraph for a university lecturer, summarizing the issues arising from the Human Genome Project. Decide whether you should quote or paraphrase the material from the text.

See Skills bank.

	A finished version of the human genome sequence became available.
	A rough draft of the human genome sequence was produced.
1	China, Germany France and Japan joined the project.
	Development of gene-targeted drugs using pharmacogenomics.
	Major investments were made in new computer technology for information processing.
	Patents had been filed on 127,000 human genes or partial human gene sequences.
	Significant investment in specialized electronic components to analyze DNA without human intervention.
	The number of base pairs sequenced reached 200 million.

As Truong VD, Sandeep KP, Cartwright GD (2007) explains that without more computers it would not be possible to achieve the stated objectives by 2005. Consequently, a large investment was made in technology which was the beginning of the science of bioinformatics. Yet, according to Truong VD, Sandeep KP, Cartwright GD (2007), they say that with less than half the project time remaining, just over 6% of the genome had been mapped. Fortunately, because they developed electronic components to analyze DNA without human intervention. Consequently, there was an enormous increase in the speed with which the genome could be mapped.

Future Medicine PloS 2007 21(5)

Implications of mapping the human genome

By Truong VD, Sandeep KP & Cartwright GD

The Human Genome Project began in 1990, following initial co-operation between the US Department of Energy and the Wellcome Trust, a UK medical charity. China, Germany, France and Japan also became full partners in the project. The objective was to generate a high-quality reference DNA sequence for the human genome. The genome represents the complete set of DNA in each organism. In humans it is made up of 3.2 billion linked segments of DNA, known as base pairs. As the activity in every cell in every living organism is governed by the DNA in its nucleus, it is clear that this project aimed to provide knowledge about the most fundamental aspects of life. By 'reading the book of life' (Searls, 2001), the project was perhaps one of the most ambitious in human history.

At that time, the project was also seen as extremely ambitious in technical terms. The laboratory techniques which were used to map the DNA were complex and time-consuming and depended on highly skilled laboratory staff. It was clear that without new technologies and techniques it would not be possible to achieve the stated objectives by 2005, so as a first step, major investments were made in computer technology for data processing. This marked the beginning of a new scientific discipline of bioinformatics, combining computing and biology. By 1998, a total of 200 million base pairs had been sequenced by the project. With less than half of the planned project time remaining, just over 6% of the genome had been mapped. Fortunately, computers were becoming cheaper and more powerful. Also by this time, significant investment had been made in developing specialized electronic components which could directly analyze the DNA without the need for human intervention. Consequently, there was an enormous increase in the speed with which the genome could be mapped.

In June 2000, a rough draft of the human genome sequence was produced. This covered 90% of the genome. Unlike the data produced by InterPro, a rival private-sector research project, the Human Genome

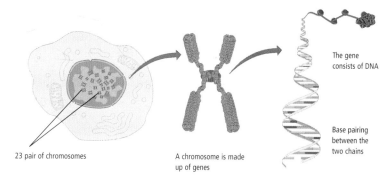

23 pair of chromosomes

A chromosome is made up of genes

The gene consists of DNA

Base pairing between the two chains

Project data was freely available to the public and could be used without any restrictions. While it was possible to access the InterPro data without charge, its use for any purpose was subject to licence agreements. This gave rise to major debates on the ethics of commercializing genome research in this way. Although InterPro was the main focus of these debates, it was not alone. Research carried out in November 2000 showed that drug and biotech companies, government institutes and universities had filed patents on 127,000 human genes or partial human gene sequences.

By April 2003, a finished version of the human genome sequence was available, along with much new knowledge. By coincidence or design, it was exactly 50 years since Watson and Crick published their paper on the structure of DNA, which identified the 'letters' of the genomic alphabet. The finished version identified all of the estimated 25,000 human genes within the genome, less than one-third fewer than expected. Around half of them were linked to a specific biological function. As a result of the project, we now know that there is only 0.1% of a difference in DNA between humans. Specific gene sequences have been associated with different diseases and disorders including breast cancer, muscle disease, deafness and blindness. DNA-based tests were among the first commercial applications of the research, and several hundred have been developed to date.

Many benefits have already emerged from this research and there will be many more over the next decade. Researchers have already begun to correlate variations in DNA with differences in results from medical interventions. This should allow us to classify individuals into subgroups, based on their DNA profile, for whom drugs could be customized. A new discipline, pharmacogenomics, is developing around the study of these interactions. The knowledge should also help tackle future pandemics and produce new developments in stem cell technologies. While these benefits are truly worthwhile, there are a number of key societal issues arising from the knowledge created by the Human Genome Project. Perhaps the most important relates to the ownership of genetic information, both at a societal and individual level. At a societal level, we have seen how InterPro sought to license genomic data to make money and while questions have been raised regarding its right to do so, it is still free to pursue commercial projects using the data. At the individual level, the issue of access to and control of data about the genetic makeup of individuals is already extremely important, given that susceptibility to many diseases has been linked to specific genes which can be identified by testing. However, as more and more aspects of what makes us human are linked to specific elements of DNA in our genes, the opportunity for misuse of this information becomes ever greater. It may be that thanks to the Human Genome Project we can now read 'the book of life', but as a society it is not yet clear what use we will make of the knowledge we find there.

A Study the words in box a.

1 Check the pronunciation and grammar.

2 What are their meanings in a research report?

> conduct data discussion findings
> implication interview interviewee
> interviewer limitation method questionnaire
> random recommendation research question
> respondent results sample survey undertake

B Read the two *Method* paragraphs on the right.

1 Copy them into your notebook. Put the verbs in brackets in the correct form.

2 Identify the original research questions and the research methods used.

C What are the sections of a research report? What order should they go in?

D Read the *Introduction* to Report A and the *Conclusion* to Report B on the opposite page.

1 Why was the research undertaken?

2 What are the elements of a good introduction and conclusion?

See Skills bank.

Report A: Method

A written questionnaire (design) to measure how ethnic minorities perceived the safety and likely societal benefits from clinical trials compared with their non-ethnic counterparts. Six hundred questionnaires (send) to a random sample of patients selected from each of the two subject groups. Two hundred and fifty (return). In addition, twenty-five patients from ethnic minorities (interview) in GP surgeries. Over 65% of the sample (be) women.

Report B: Method

In order to find out what the main issues surrounding the level of participation by ethnic minorities in clinical trials are, a literature search (undertake) using the PubMed database and the Google search engine. The search terms which (use) were *ethnic minority*, *participate* and *clinical trial*.

A Describe the data in Figures 1 and 2.

B Look at the first paragraph from the *Findings* section of Report A.

1 Complete the spaces with quantity phrases. Put the verbs in the correct tense.

2 Write another paragraph, using Figures 1 and 2.

C Look at the *Literature search notes* on page 99.

1 Rearrange the items in the *Context* column so they match with the issues.

2 Link each issue identified with the relevant ethical principles listed below. (There may be more than one answer.)

- autonomy
- beneficence
- justice
- non-malfeasance

Report A: Findings

Firstly, a _____ (30%) of ethnic respondents (state) that they were unlikely to agree to take part in a clinical trial if asked. In addition, the _____ (60%) (say) they were likely to agree and a _____ (10%) had no opinion. The results from the non-ethnic sample were similar. Finally, a _____ (70%) (indicate) that they were likely to participate, while a _____ (30%) of non-ethnic respondents (feel) it was unlikely they would want to be involved.

D Write a discusion paragraph for Report B using the ideas from the *Literature search notes* on page 99.

Report A: Introduction

There has been much debate about the level of participation by ethnic minorities in clinical trials.

It is important that ethnic minorities are adequately represented in clinical trials, as otherwise the result may not provide a true picture of the effectiveness and safety of the drug across the whole population.

This report will describe a survey undertaken to examine the differences in perception of clinical trials between individuals from ethnic minorities and those from non-ethnic minorities. Recommendations will be made on how recruitment of volunteers among ethnic minorities can be improved.

Report B: Conclusion

To conclude, it appears that the main problems in recruiting ethnic minority members are those which also affect the non-ethnic community. For example, a considerable number may be unable to read English.

The evidence suggests that cultural issues should be taken into account when obtaining consent from ethnic minority patients to participate in clinical trials. More emphasis should be put on face-to-face discussion. Where possible, a qualified translator should be used and the family should be encouraged to ask questions.

The underrepresentation of ethnic minorities in clinical trils is likely to continue if the implementation of these recommendations is delayed.

Speedy implementations should see the erosion of many of the identified barriers.

Report A

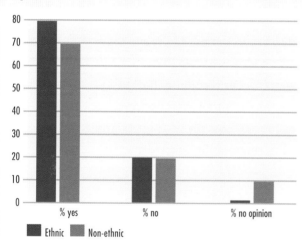

Q. Do you think clinical trials are necessary for the development of new drugs?

Figure 1: *Perception of need for clinical trials*

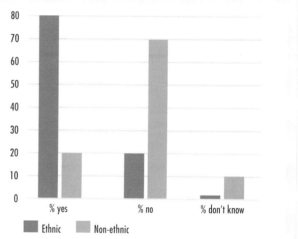

Q. Do you think new drugs are less likely to benefit ethnic minority members?

Figure 2: *Perception of benefits of new drugs to ethnic minorities*

Report B

Literature search notes on perceptions of patients from ethnic minorities on participation in clinical trials

Issues identified	Context
1 Disclosure	A patients often only make decisions as part of larger family unit
2 Poor literacy	B may not understand concepts such as randomization and may be unable to evaluate amount of risk in trial
3 Family-centred culture	C often non-English speakers; many with low literacy levels in native language also
4 Lack of perceived relevance	D believe new drugs less likely to benefit ethnic minorities
5 Poor understanding of research methodology	E in many cultures traditional to tell family diagnosis/prognosis, not patient; patient may not know they have specific condition
6 Inequality of outcome	F not clear what benefit of trial is to them or their patient group; unaware of the broader implications of trial outcomes

Introductory verbs

Choosing the right introductory verb is important. Your choice of introductory verb shows what kind of statement the writer is making.

Example:
Findless (2007, p.6) argues that mortality is affected by factors other than national wealth.
Your choice of introductory verb also shows what you think of another writer's ideas. This is an important part of academic work.

Example:
Braines and Kahn (2008, p.13) claim that recent research into the human genome gives us a vital weapon to fight future pandemics.

Verb	The writer ...
agree	thinks this idea from someone else is true
accept, concede	reluctantly thinks this idea from someone else is true
consider, emphasize, note, observe, point out, state, suggest*	is giving his/her opinion
argue, assert, claim, contend, insist	is giving an opinion that others may not agree with
cite	is referring to someone else's ideas
disagree, dispute	thinks an idea is wrong
suggest*	is giving his/her recommendation
describe	is giving a definition/description
illustrate, indicate, show	is explaining, possibly with an example
report	is giving research findings

*suggest can have two meanings

Linking ideas in a text

Linking words, which join ideas within a sentence or between sentences, convey different meanings.

	Within sentences	Between sentences
Contrast	*but, whereas, while*	*However, In/By contrast, On the other hand*
Concession	*although, despite/ in spite of the fact that*	*However, At the same time, Nevertheless, Despite/In spite of + noun, Yet*
Result	*so, so that*	*So, As a result, Consequently, Therefore*
Reason	*because, since, as*	*Because of + noun, Owing to + noun, Due to + noun*

Referring to quantities and group sizes in a report

		majority	
A/An	*overwhelming/large/significant slight/small/insignificant/tiny*	*minority*	
		number	*(of + noun)*
Over		*half*	
More	*than*	*a quarter a third*	
Less		*x%*	

Structuring a research report

A research report is an account of some research which has been undertaken to find out about a situation or a phenomenon, e.g., *What do members of ethnic minorities feel about taking part in clinical trials?*

• Introduction	introduce topic; background information; reasons for research
• Methods	research questions; how research was carried out
• Findings/results	answers to research questions
• Discussion	issues arising from findings; limitations of research
• Conclusion	summary of main findings; implications; recommendations; possibilities for further research

Writing introductions and conclusions

Introduction

- Introduce the topic of the report.
- Say why the topic is important.
- Give background information.
- Give an outline of the report plan.

Note: No substantial information; this belongs in the body of the report.

Conclusion

- Summarize the main points in the report without repeating unnecessarily.
- Make some concluding comments such as likely implications or recommendations.

Note: No new information; all the main points should be in the body of the report.

Deciding when to quote and when to paraphrase

When referring to sources, you will need to decide whether to quote directly or to paraphrase/summarize.

- **Quote** when the writer's words are special or show a particularly clever use of language. This is often the case with strongly stated *definitions* or *opinions.*
- **Paraphrase/summarize** descriptions and factual information.

Incorporating quotations

- Use an introductory verb.
- Don't forget the quotation marks.
- Make the quotes fit the grammar of the sentence.
- Show any missing words with '...'.

- Copy the original words exactly.
- Add emphasis with italics and write [emphasis added].
- Add words which are not in the original but are necessary to fully understand the quotation out of context. Put the extra word(s) in brackets.

Do not quote more than one sentence **within the body** of a paragraph. If you want to quote two or three sentences, put a colon and write the quote as indented text, so that it clearly stands out from the body of your essay.

However, think very carefully before you include a long quote. It is usually better to paraphrase in this case.

Additional material

5.3 Symbols and abbreviations for notes

Symbols

&, +	and, plus
−	less, minus
±	plus or minus
=	is, equals, is the same as
≈	is approximately equivalent to
≠	is not, is not the same as, doesn't mean, does not equal, is different from
>	is greater than, is more than, is over
<	is less than
→	gives, produces, leads to, results in
←	is given by, is produced by, results from, comes from
↑	rises, increases, grows
↓	falls, decreases, declines
"	ditto (repeats text immediately above)
∴	therefore, so
	because, as, since
@	at
C	century, as in 20th C
§	paragraph
#	number, as in #1
?	this is doubtful

Abbreviations

e.g.	for example
c.	approximately, as in c.1900
cf.	compare
Ch.	chapter
ed./eds.	editor(s)
et al.	and the other people (used when referring to a book with more than one author)
etc.	and all the rest
ff.	and the following, as in p.10ff.
fig.	figure (used when giving a title to a drawing or table)
i.e.	that is, that means, in other words
ibid.	in the same place in the source already mentioned
NB	important
n.d.	no date given
No., no.	number
op. cit	in the source already mentioned
p.	page
pp.	pages, as in pp.1–10
re.	concerning
ref.	with reference to
viz.	namely
vol.	volume

5.4
Student A
	1 Secondary
	
	= info from sources, e.g., journals, books, organizational reports on
	      the Internet
	      (i.e., already exists)
	
	+ cheap; good overview of diseases; relatively fast
	
	− reports ⟶ poss. out of date, data not in required format

5.4 **Student B**	**2 Primary** = new info: from observation, use of questionnaires, etc. + info = recent; can ask specific questions (good method for psych. research) − expensive; time-consuming

5.4 **Student C**	**3 Qualitative** $\neq$ numbers; used to find out attitudes, beliefs, etc. Methods inc. interviews, group discussions, etc. $+$ can get much better understanding of effects of disease, transmission patterns, possibilities to prevent transmission $-$ because of small numbers difficult to generalize, ideally need to be used in conjunction with quantitative methods

5.4 **Student D**	**4 Quantitative** $=$ statistical info, from recorded incidents or questionnaires $+$ good for factual info; overview of trends $\therefore$ large nos. $-$ relatively little insight into broader effects of disease or transmission patterns

7.4
Student A

Alternative to acute care   1 Specialist centres

- Good example is a Stroke Centre which houses stroke specialists and relevant equipment.
- This equipment and level of specialization is not always available in local hospitals.
- Stroke victims need to be treated within an hour – risk of delays in overcrowded A&E.
- 100,000 strokes in UK and 750,000 in USA every year.
- Ageing population means numbers are going to increase dramatically.

7.4
Student B

Alternative to acute care   2 Minor injuries units

- Open 24 hours a day, 7 days a week. Treat minor complaints such as sprains, etc.
- Run by nurse practitioners with a two-year degree course in advanced nursing.
- Overseen by general practitioners.
- Follow up by referral to A&E if necessary.
- Some have their own fracture clinics, which also takes strain off A&E.

7.4 **Student C**	Alternative to acute care 3 Cycle paramedics
	· Paramedics travel by bicycle and therefore have access to urbanized areas which are difficult to reach by ambulance because of heavy traffic.
	· Able to be right at the patient's side with all the equipment.
	· Cycle carries: oxygen cylinder for pain relief, observations bag, first aid kit, etc.
	· Much cheaper than sending out rapid response unit (ambulance).
	· Paramedic can administer first aid and take vital signs before ambulance arrives.
	· Follow up by referral to A&E if necessary.

7.4 **Student D**	Alternative to acute care 4 Air ambulance services
	• Rural areas can be reached quickly and ambulances transport patients directly to specialist hospitals or the nearest A&E.
	• Able to carry out at-the-scene and en-route treatment.
	• Team includes the pilot, paramedic and sometimes a nurse.
	• Equipment carried includes respirators, medication, an ECG and monitoring unit, CPR equipment and stretchers.
	• Air ambulance services rely on public donations and are not part of the NHS in England and Wales (in Scotland they are state-run).

11.2 Model Cornell notes

Review	Notes
	Background to current ethico-legal framework
	· X NOT linked to 4th C Hippocratic Oath
	starting point for development medico-legal ethics today:
	Nuremberg Code 1945
	· experiments ⟶ 2WW prisoners (ice water to test survival)
	· Code clarifies what is acceptable in experiments with humans
	· principle of voluntary subject consent
	(no guidance on patient-doctor relationship)
	Declaration of Helsinki 1964 (WMA)
	· addresses doctor-patient relationship
	· participation voluntary AND informed
	⟶ need for informed consent from all patients
	· basis for current medico-legal ethics
	Consent in practice - differences
	· some doctors view consent as strictly legal ⟶ avoid legal action for assault
	· some think only doctors can make informed decision Not agree. Legal and ethical reasons (patient autonomy)
	Consent form
	· Sudore et al. (2006) - 28% patients fully understand form 1st time ⟶ need to check patient understanding
	· ! CANNOT assume patient understanding ⟶ important issue for legislators
	Practical issues
	· check patient can legally give consent -adults OK if reason not impaired
	(unable to give consent e.g., drink/drugs/mental illness)
	children - not poss in US, OK in UK/Can/Oz if pass 'Gillick standard' (mature enough to give consent).
Summary	

Wordlist

Note: Where a word has more than one part of speech, this is indicated in brackets. The part of speech given is that of the word as it is used in the unit. So, for example, *set* is listed as *set (v)*, although it can also be a noun.

	Unit		Unit		Unit
A		benefit	8	contaminant	6
(patient) admissions	7	benefits	12	control	9
abdomen	3	biochemistry	1	control group	10
abnormality	6	bioinformatics	12	correlate	12
access (n and v)	4	biomedical research	11	customize	12
accredited	7	biopsy	6		
active ingredient	10	blinding	10	**D**	
acute care	7	breakthrough	2	data	10
administer	1	breastbone	3	data protection	11
admissions	1	browse	4	database	4
admit	7	bypass	2	decision	11
adverse	6, 8			decline (n and v)	5
advice	8			decrease (n and v)	5
Alexandria Plan	7	**C**		degenerative	5
allergy	8	cancer	8	demographic	5
anaesthetic	6	capillary	3	department	7
analgesic	6, 8	cardiac	2, 5	detect	8
analyse	1	cardiovascular	3	developed	5
analysis	1	care cycle	7	diabetes	8
analyze	5	cell	1	diagnose	1
anatomical	6	characteristic	6	diagnosis	5, 7, 8
anatomy	1, 3	characteristics	2, 5	dietician	8
anterior	3	chromosome	12	digestive	3
antiviral	6	circulation	2	dignity	11
artery	3	clinic	8	discharge	7
autonomic	6	clinical justification	11	discomfort	8
autonomy	11	clinical study/trial	11	disease	1, 8
		collagen	3	document	4
		commercialize	12	donate	12
B		communicable	5	double-blind	10
bacteria	6	compliance	11	drop (n and v)	5
barrier contraceptive	9	confidentiality	11	dysfunction	12
base pair	12	conflict of interest	11		
behaviour	8	congenital	5		
behavioural disorder	7	congestive	2	**E**	
benchmark	9	consent	11	eliminate	6
beneficence	11	contagious	5	elimination	9

	Unit		Unit		Unit
Emergency Medicine	7	history	1	**L**	
emphysema	9	hospital ward	7	lateral	3
encode	12	human rights	9	legal regulation	11
environmental	5	humans	12	legislation	9
epidemic	9	hyperlink	4	lifestyle modification	8
eradication	2, 5, 9	hypothermic	2	limb	3
ethical (principle)	11			lipid	6
ethnic origin	9			log in/log on	4
evidence	10	**I**		log off	4
examine	8	identifiable	5		
exercise	8	identify	1	**M**	
exposure	9	illness	1	malfunction	1
		immunity	2	management	8
		immunization	8	management (of a condition)	7
F		incidence	5, 8	maternal	5
false positive	8	increase (n and v)	5	maternal mortality	9
family planning	9	incubation period	2	measures	9
fatal	2, 9	infant mortality	9	mechanism	1
fatality	2	infection	8	mechanisms	2
fatigue	8	infectious	5, 9	medial	3
forearm	3	inferior	3	medical progress	11
fracture	7	inflammatory	5	menu	4
functioning	1	information	11	meta-analysis	10
		informed consent	11	metabolic	6
		inherited	12	microbiology	1
G		injection	8	middle-income	9
gain	11	inoculation	8	migraine	8
gastrointestinal	3	interpret	1	minimize	8
gene	12	intervals	8	minor injury	7
goal	2, 12	intervention	10, 11	molecular	6, 12
gradual	5	interview	5	monitoring	8
growth	5	irregular	1	moral right	11
				mortality	2, 5, 9
H		**J**		multi-centre study	11
heal	1	jab	8	mutation	12
health	1	justice	11		
health hazard	9				
health risk	9	**K**		**N**	
heart	2	keyword	4	nausea	8
heat stroke	9			neoplastic	5
heatwave	9			non-communicable	5
hereditary	5				

	Unit		Unit
stem	12	**V**	
stem cell	12	vaccination	8
stigma	12	vaccine	2
substance	6	validate	10
superficial	3	valve	2
superior	3	variant	12
surgery	2, 8	vascular	8
survey (n and v)	5	vector-borne	9
sympathize	8	vein	3
symptoms	2	ventricle	3
syringe	8	vertebrae	3
systematic reviews	10	vessel	3
		virus	6
T		vital signs	7
teaching hospital	7		
technique	2	**W**	
telemedicine	4	waiting room	7
telesurgery	4	work-related	9
temperature	2		
theatre	1		
therapeutic	6		
tissue	2, 6		
toxic	6		
toxicology	6		
transmission	2, 5, 9		
transplant	2		
treat	1		
treatment	6, 8		
treatment group	10		
triage nurse	7		
triage room	7		
trial	12		
trial design	10		
trunk	3		
U			
username/ID	4		

Transcripts

Unit 1, Lesson 1.2, Exercise B 🎧 1.1

Part 1

Good morning and welcome to the Faculty of Medicine. As Dean of the Faculty, it gives me great pleasure to see so many of you here today preparing to undertake the Bachelor of Medicine and Surgery degree course. The successful completion of the course will lead to a career as a doctor, one of the most rewarding and demanding careers it is possible to have. Your training will range from exploring the structure of cells to learning about medical codes of conduct.

So, what does it mean to study medicine? The word medicine comes to us from the Latin, mederi – to heal, which is at the core of medicine. There are many branches of medicine, but all have something in common. They all seek to heal, from dermatology, which tries to heal the skin, to psychiatry, which tries to heal the mind.

Unit 1, Lesson 1.2, Exercise C 🎧 1.2

Part 2

So let's talk about some of the core subjects you will study in your first year. Bear in mind that these can be different subjects, depending on whether the university is following a traditional model, as we are, or has combined pre-clinical and clinical studies, as other universities have.

You will begin with human anatomy, which looks at the structure of the body. This will help you to understand physiology – the way the healthy body functions. The next area of study is pharmacology – the study of how drugs interact with living organisms. In biochemistry, the chemistry which takes place in living organisms, you will analyze the structure and function of their chemical compounds. Finally, you will learn about specific diseases in pathology, how they are caused and how to cure them. These are the core subjects that you will study, and there will be others.

Unit 1, Lesson 1.2, Exercise D 🎧 1.3

Part 3

You may find it difficult to absorb so many new words at the same time. I must stress that you will be introduced to a whole new language as you continue your study of medicine. However, it may help if you realize that some words which are used in medicine are already in common use in English. Though the meaning when the word is used in medicine may change, it still retains some of the original meaning.

A good example of this is the word scan. In everyday English it is used to refer to the way in which a person looks around quickly for something, or reads quickly, looking for specific information. In a medical context, the word is used for the use of ultrasound to provide a visual display of the internal organs and other body structures. In both contexts the word indicates a means of finding information visually.

Another example of this is the word cell. In general English this usually refers to a small room, as in a prison cell, where somebody is locked up. In a medical context it is the smallest unit of a living organism. The connection between the two words here is much less clear. However, both come from the Latin word cella, meaning small room. The prison cell is a small room within a bigger building and the cell can be seen as a small room within the overall structure of its organism.

Unit 1, Lesson 1.2, Exercise E 🎧 1.4

Part 4

I'd like to look a little more closely now at the subjects you will study, starting with human anatomy, which is my special interest. It is the study of the outward appearance of the structures of the human body. There are two sub-divisions that we refer to as gross anatomy and microscopic anatomy. In gross anatomy we will study those structures of the body that can be seen with the naked eye.

In microscopic anatomy you will use microscopes to study the anatomical structures at a much more detailed level. As part of this you will have an introduction to histology (the study of the organization of tissues) and to cytology (the study of the structure of cells). You will also have an opportunity to gain an introduction to histopathology, the study of disease in cells, which you will study in more detail during the clinical component of your course.

Pharmacology is another area which may be new to you. This is the study of drugs, what they are, how they work and what they do. You will look at how the functions of organisms and live tissues are modified by chemical substances. You should not confuse it with pharmacy, which is concerned with the scientific, legal and managerial aspects of providing medicines to patients.

Unit 1, Lesson 1.3, Exercise E 🎧 1.5

Introduction 1

Today I'm going to talk about the advantages and disadvantages of two different types of surgery that we can use to deal with cancers in the body. Until relatively recently, all operations to remove cancer were carried out using a scalpel, which is a sharp instrument, or type of knife. The scalpel is used to cut open the skin and tissue surrounding the tumour, and then to remove the tumour itself. In recent years, however, laser surgery has started to replace traditional surgery for removing some types of tumour.

Introduction 2

The purpose of today's lecture is to look at some major landmarks in the developments of medicine. The traditional starting point for the history of our profession is the Greeks. There were many notable Greek physicians, perhaps the best known being Hippocrates. His book on medicine, written around 400 BC, was of great significance to modern medicine. It stated that the well-being of the patient should be the central concern of the doctor and this forms a core part of the Hippocratic Oath, which forms the basis of many medical codes of practice today.

Introduction 3

In the lecture today, I'm going to talk about the different stages of Alzheimer's and how these can be recognized in the patient. Alzheimer's is a disease which affects mental, cognitive and motor ability and ultimately often leads to the death of the patient. It also causes considerable distress to the patient themselves and to their carers. There are five distinctive stages to Alzheimer's and we will now look at each of these stages in turn.

Introduction 4

The purpose of the lecture today is to look at how a doctor used his powers of observation to find the solution to a problem that was affecting his patients. The year was 1854 and the doctor was Dr John Snow, a general practitioner based in

London. The problem was that an increasing number of his patients were contracting cholera. This was a disease which was fatal, sometimes within hours, and for which there was no cure at the time. In order to solve the problem, he conducted a range of different investigations.

Introduction 5

The function of the endocrine system is to regulate the various organs within the body and it does this primarily by using hormones, which are produced by glands in the body. Today we are going to look at ways in which the endocrine system can malfunction and the effects that that can produce. I would like to begin by looking at the functioning of the thyroid gland. This is one of the largest glands in the body and it is located in the neck, below the mouth. It produces a number of hormones, the most important of which are T4 and T3.

Unit 1, Lesson 1.4, Exercise E 🎧 1.6

Lecture 1

So, what exactly is a laser? Well, a laser is a light of very high intensity which can be focused in an extremely precise way. Because of its intensity, it can burn whatever it is focused on. This means that it is particularly suited for cancers which occur on the surface of the body or the lining of internal organs. In contrast to using a scalpel, where the surrounding tissue is cut away to get to the tumour, a laser can be used through an endoscope. An endoscope is a flexible tube inserted into an opening in the body, which is manipulated so that it gets close to the location of the tumour without the need for additional cutting.

So, let's look at the advantages of laser surgery. Because lasers are more precise, they cause less bleeding and damage to normal tissue than standard surgical tools. As a result, patients tend to bleed less, to have less pain and swelling and there are lower levels of scarring. In addition, operations using a laser are usually shorter than traditional operations and can sometimes be done on an outpatient basis. All of these factors mean that there is a much lower risk of infection for the patient.

However, laser therapy has some limitations. Firstly, surgeons who use this technique must have extra specialized training before they are allowed to use the equipment, and much stricter precautions must be followed. Secondly, the equipment required to carry out the operation is expensive and bulky. Thirdly, additional technical assistance may also be required for the maintenance of the equipment. A final limitation is that as the surgery may need to be repeated.

Unit 1, Lesson 1.4, Exercise E 🎧 1.7

Lecture 2

Following on from the Greeks, the Romans were responsible for many new developments in medicine. The work of Galen, born around 120 AD, is of particular significance, as he developed models of the body and how it functions. These were accepted for over twelve hundred years.

The publication of a book by William Harvey in 1628, describing the circulation of blood in the body, could be seen as the next landmark stage of development, essentially marking the basis of modern physiology. Along with the developments in chemistry, which took place around the same time, this meant that the body could be studied rationally as a functioning system for the first time.

Another significant development was the discovery of vaccination. This was in use in England from the 1730s. Children were deliberately infected with small amounts of smallpox so that they would develop a resistance to the disease. Unfortunately, this could sometimes be fatal. The process was refined in 1796, when Edward Jenner discovered that cowpox (a non-fatal disease) could provide immunity to smallpox (which was fatal). Further developments came in the 1870s when Louis Pasteur was able to produce weak strains of viruses in the laboratory and develop vaccines for anthrax.

The introduction of antiseptics by Joseph Lister in 1865 gave medicine another tool with which to fight infection. Maintenance of good levels of hygiene had long been recognized as important in preventing illness, but Lister outlined the mechanisms by which infection could spread in a clinical setting and introduced carbolic acid as an effective way of preventing this. His work led to the widespread acceptance of the theory that micro-organisms caused disease.

Finally, I'd like to mention the significant development in the fight against micro-organisms with the discovery of penicillin, which is usually attributed to Alexander Fleming. While the action of penicillin on bacteria was known about from 1928 onward, it was not until 1942 that it was first used successfully on a patient. Its success in treating a very wide range of diseases meant that, for perhaps the first time, doctors had a tool which was easy to use and which could quickly bring about enormous improvements in a patient's condition. The modern era of medicine had dawned.

Unit 1, Lesson 1.4, Exercise E 🎧 1.8

Lecture 3

In stage one of the disease, the changes are very similar to those which occur with the onset of old age. For example, short memory lapses, mild word aphasia – I mean, not being able to think of the correct word – not being able to find everyday items such as glasses and keys. Even though the individual notices some decline in cognition, it is not noticed by those around them. At this stage, Alzheimer's is very rarely diagnosed.

Stage two of progression is marked by a significant decline in memory function and the beginnings of a personality change. There is difficulty in remembering the names of new acquaintances, difficulty in remembering items which have been read, and difficulties in organizing and planning. Towards the end of this stage, the symptoms become more and more evident to others around the individual. A small proportion of individuals are diagnosed with Alzheimer's at this stage.

By stage three of the disease, individuals are unable to function without assistance. There is great difficulty in remembering information such as their address and phone number, and sometimes even the date, day of the week or month. While they may be able to remember the names of people near to them, they forget the names of those they see on a less regular basis. They may often not recognize their surroundings. By this stage, a significant proportion of patients will be diagnosed.

In stage four, patients will require help with most of their daily functions. Personality changes also become evident and there may be expressions of inappropriate emotions. Patients can still distinguish between familiar and unfamiliar faces, but have difficulty in identification. They can wander off and get lost, if not kept under observation. Frequently, they may need help with their bodily functions and can become doubly incontinent. They appear lost and confused for most of the time, though there may be periods of lucidity.

The final stage of the disease is characterised by a catatonic-like state, which means that patients are unable to speak or respond to others, though they may occasionally utter words. Their muscles become rigid and they are unable to sit up, smile, swallow or hold their heads up. Death eventually intervenes, typically around eight years after the initial diagnosis of Alzheimer's.

Unit 1, Lesson 1.4, Exercise E 🎧 1.9

Lecture 4

The problem that Dr Snow faced was that he did not know what was causing the disease. At this time, the dominant theory regarding the transmission of disease was that it came from breathing foul air or 'miasma' which contained harmful particles. Dr Snow, on the other hand, felt that the water which people drank might be making them ill. However, he was unable to describe the mechanism which caused it, because the micro-organism theory of disease would not be fully formulated until 1875.

He had a number of scientific tools at his disposal to help identify the cause of the problem. He took samples of the water from all the pumps in the area and investigated them using a microscope and chemical analysis. However, this did not reveal anything of significance. His next step was to identify where the people who died of cholera had lived and he created a spot map to show this. The results of the spot map showed that most of the people who died lived very close to one of the public water pumps, on Broad Street. Another, smaller cluster was close to another public water pump.

Snow followed this up by talking to the residents who lived near the second pump. He found that people who had died there drank water from the Broad Street pump, as they preferred the taste. As a result of this he concluded that the water from the Broad Street pump was a common factor in all the deaths. He took his results to the local authorities, and as a result of his investigations the handle was taken off the pump, so that no more water could be taken from that source. The outbreak came to an end shortly afterwards.

Even though he was unable to identify the mechanism which caused the disease, Dr Snow was successful in preventing it. This investigation laid the foundations of the science of epidemiology,

the study of the transmission of diseases in populations. The science still relies on many of the techniques pioneered by Dr Snow, particularly the use of statistics to identify the spread of a disease among a population, and hence its likely sources. It has also given rise to the branch of medicine known as public health medicine, which has delivered many of the enormous gains in life expectancy and quality of life experienced over the last century.

Unit 1, Lesson 1.4, Exercise E 🎧 1.10

Lecture 5

These hormones control how quickly the body metabolizes energy. They also have direct effects on most organs, including the heart, which beats faster and harder under the influence of thyroid hormones. Essentially all cells in the body will respond to increases in thyroid hormone with an increase in the rate at which they conduct their business.

In healthy people, the thyroid makes just the right amounts of T4 and T3. However, in a relatively small number of people there can be an imbalance of the hormones. Hyperthyroidism is the condition which is caused by the effects of too much of the thyroid hormones on tissues of the body. Hypothyroidism is the condition caused by too little of the thyroid hormones reaching the tissues.

For the moment we will focus on the effects of hyperthyroidism. While there can be many reasons for patients to develop hyperthyroidism, most of the symptoms they experience are the same whatever the cause.

So, what are these symptoms? Because the body uses energy more quickly, patients can often feel hotter than normal and, even though they may be eating more than normal. can lose weight because their metabolism is much higher. Patients usually complain of fatigue, but this is combined with insomnia that can make them very irritable and easily upset. They may also develop irregular heartbeats (palpitations) and trembling of the hands. In severe cases patients can suffer shortness of breath, chest pain, and muscle weakness.

Because the symptoms can develop gradually, many patients do not realize that they are sick for weeks or months after the onset of the symptoms. Older people may display few or none of the typical symptoms of hyperthyroidism and may just lose weight or become depressed.

Unit 3, Lesson 3.2, Exercise B 🎧 1.11

Part 1

If we're all here, we'll make a start.

What we're going to look at today is human physiology. So what is physiology? Well, it deals with the functioning of the body and its internal organs; essentially it's the science of the mechanical, physical, and biochemical functioning of a human in good health. We will look at levels of structural organization within the human body: molecular, cellular, tissue, organ, system and organismal – the body, in other words. We can identify 11 separate systems. I'll take you through these and then we'll concentrate on two and look at them in a little more detail: firstly the skeletal system and then the cardiovascular. The aim of today's lecture is for you to start developing an understanding of the functioning of the body.

Unit 3, Lesson 3.2, Exercise C 🎧 1.12

Part 2

You will already have an idea of some of the systems of the body from your own knowledge: the skeletal system, for example; the muscular and nervous systems. There are 11 in total, but today I'm going to be focusing on just two.

Firstly, the skeletal system. Most of you will be familiar with the arrangement of bones within the human skeleton. Believe it or not, bone is a living tissue which is constantly being renewed and reshaped, with new bone being built up while old bone is broken down. The structure of bone is made up of around 25 per cent water, 25 per cent collagen and 50 per cent crystallized mineral salts. The mineral salts give bone its hardness and the collagen fibres give it flexibility.

Bones can be divided into four types. Short bones are nearly equal in length and width. Most ankle and wrist bones are short bones. Long bones have a greater length than their width. They include those in the thigh, leg and arm. Flat bones are thin in shape and these include the breastbone, ribs and shoulder blades. Irregular bones have shapes which do not fall into the other categories and include bones in the face and the vertebrae of the backbone.

Unit 3, Lesson 3.2, Exercise D 🎧 1.13

Part 3

The cardiovascular system is made up of three components: blood, the heart and the blood vessels. The function of the system is to transport blood throughout the body, with the heart acting as the pump for circulation.

Blood is essential for the functioning of the body. It transports oxygen from the lungs to the cells throughout the body and takes carbon dioxide from the cells to the lungs. It also carries nutrients and hormones. Blood is also important in regulating body temperature. Blood is made up of plasma, red and white blood cells, and platelets. Red blood cells are responsible for transporting the oxygen from the lungs to cells throughout the body. There are about 250 million red blood cells in a drop of blood. White blood cells protect the body against disease, forming a first line of defence against infection. The ratio of red blood cells to white blood cells is around 700 to 1. Platelets are the component of blood which helps to stop bleeding when blood vessels are damaged. There are between 500,000 and 2 million platelets in each drop of blood.

The heart is the mechanism by which the blood is pumped through the body. It beats about 100,000 times each day, pumping more than 14,000 litres of blood. The left side of the heart pumps blood through the blood vessels. The right side pumps blood through the lungs to collect oxygen and discharge carbon dioxide. As you can see from slide 4, the heart is composed of four chambers; the right and left atria and the left and right ventricles. Blood passes through valves in the heart which prevent the blood from flowing backwards. The heart is made up of muscle fibres and has its own blood supply. About one per cent of the fibres have specialized functions which allow them to coordinate the actions of the heart.

There are three main types of blood vessels: arteries, veins and capillaries. Arteries carry the blood away from the heart to body tissues. These divide into smaller and smaller arteries, eventually forming microscopic vessels called capillaries. The capillaries are known as exchange vessels because they allow the exchange of nutrients and waste between the body's cells and the blood. The capillaries come together to eventually form veins which are the blood vessels transporting blood back to the heart.

Unit 3, Lesson 3.2, Exercise E 🎧 1.14

Part 4

So, to summarize, we've looked briefly at the 11 systems in the body and we looked at two of them in more detail – the skeletal system and the cardiovascular system. Anatomy and physiology are closely related fields of study: anatomy is the study of form while physiology is the study of function. They are intrinsically tied and it is usual to study them in tandem as part of the medical curriculum. OK, that's it for today. Next time we'll look at anatomy as a basic principle. Don't forget to do a bit of research on it before you come. Thanks for listening today.

Unit 3, Lesson 3.2, Exercise F 🎧 1.15

1 Bone tissue is made up of collagen, mineral salts and water.

2 Blood transports carbon dioxide from the lungs to the heart.

3 The heart pumps 40,000 litres of blood around the body every day.

4 There is a higher ratio of red to white blood cells.

5 The three main types of blood vessel are arteries, capillaries and veins.

6 Wrist bones are always equal in length and width.

Unit 3, Lesson 3.3, Exercise A 🎧 1.16

1 cardio'vascular

2 repro'ductive

3 me'chanical

4 re'spiratory

5 bio'chemical

6 'hormone

7 'artery

8 'regulate

9 di'gestive

10 'organ

11 in'ternal

12 circu'lation

13 'nutrient

14 'nervous

15 'system

16 'vessel

17 'skeleton

18 re'new

Unit 3, Lesson 3.4, Exercise A 🎧 1.17

Part 1

In the last lecture we talked about physiology. Physiology, if you remember, deals with the functioning of the body of a healthy human and its internal organs. There is a close link between human physiology and the principle we are going to look at today – anatomy. So, while physiology deals with the functions of the body, human anatomy is the science of structure within the body and the relationship of those structures to each other. More precisely, we'll look at how we describe the positioning of the different regions of the body, as well as the relations between them.

Unit 3, Lesson 3.4, Exercise C 🎧 1.18

Part 2

The language used in anatomy is very precise, so that the location of specific parts of the body in relation to each other can be indicated quickly and clearly. When describing body parts it is taken for granted that the body is positioned in a standard way, known as the anatomical position. We can see this very clearly in the first slide. When a body is in the anatomical position it is standing erect. facing the observer. The head is level and the eyes are facing forward. Feet are flat on the floor, pointing forward and the hands are at the sides with the palms facing forward. This standard position means that the relationship between the different parts of the body is always the same.

Unit 3, Lesson 3.4, Exercise D 🎧 1.19

Part 3

How then do we describe the body in anatomical terms? Looking at slide 2, we can see it is divided into five main regions. These are the head, neck, trunk, upper limbs and lower limbs. The divisions between the regions are fairly straightforward. The neck attaches the head to the trunk. The trunk is made up of the chest, abdomen and pelvis. The upper limbs are attached to the trunk. So that's head connected by the neck to the trunk, and the upper limbs connected to the trunk. The upper limbs consist of the shoulders, arms, forearms, wrists and hands. These elements are on either side, of course. So that's the upper limbs. The lower limbs attach to the trunk at the groin and are made up of the buttocks, legs, ankles and feet.

OK. We've seen the five main regions and the descriptions of the regions, but as we mentioned before it is important to be able to describe the relationship between the various body parts. In order to do this, we need to use standard directional terms to describe the relative position of the various body parts. For example, take a look at slide 3; here you see the sternum – or breastbone. It is in front of the lungs – in anatomical terms – anterior to them. Or, to put it another way, the lungs are posterior to the sternum. From this you can see that the posterior and anterior are opposite in meaning – behind and in front. You can also see that the heart is above the stomach. In anatomical terms it is superior to the stomach, or the stomach is inferior to the heart.

In the final slide you can see the same terms or anatomical planes quite clearly: superior, inferior, etc. But, as you can see, there are others. Medial indicates a location towards the centre of the body, and lateral indicates one towards either side of the body. Proximal indicates the body part is nearer to the attachment of a limb to the trunk, and distal indicates it is further away. Finally, where a part is nearer the surface of the body it is referred to as superficial while deep refers to a position away from the surface of the body. Sometimes it is necessary to describe the absolute position of the organs in the body, rather than their relationship to other organs. To do this we use the three anatomical planes. These are imaginary lines which cut the body into segments or parts. The frontal plane passes through both ears, dividing the body in two pieces vertically, from front to back. The lateral plane passes through the nose, dividing the body, again vertically, in the other direction, into two halves – left and right. The transverse plane passes through the waist, dividing the body horizontally from top to bottom. This allows us to establish the exact position of an organ relative to the planes. Are there any questions at this stage? No? OK.

Unit 3, Lesson 3.4, Exercise E 🎧 1.20

Part 4

So, to recap, we have been looking at the structures of the human body and their relationship to each other. So far, we have looked at the anatomical position, the anatomical planes and the regions of the body, as well as the terminology relative to these that you will be employing in your studies and with your colleagues later on in your clinical practice. On a final note, it is interesting to know that anatomical planes are also used in more advanced areas of medicine – they are frequently used in CT and MRI scans to enable doctors to visualize muscle, bone, lung and other soft tissues as well as pathologies or disease. Anyway, I'd like to finish there for now, so thank you for participating today.

Unit 5, Lesson 5.2, Exercise B 🎧 1.21

Part 1

Good morning, everyone. This morning we're going to look at disease, its causes and effects. In this first talk I'm just going to give you an overview of a few key concepts; in your seminars and assignments you'll be able to cover all the important points in more detail. So ... er ... let's see – yes – to start with, we need to consider firstly what disease is. In other words, how can we identify what we mean by a disease? And secondly, why is disease so important and how can we fight it? After that I'll talk about the global context of disease, because the worldwide distribution of particular diseases differs, along with the effects. Part of this involves analyzing population groups. So, then I'll discuss some future predictions for the incidence of disease and I'll finish by mentioning the different tools we can use to make these kinds of predictions.

Disease occurs when there are variations in normal structure or function of the body, causing problems or discomfort to the patient. Disease can be caused by external (also called environmental) factors, or genetic or other internal factors. Internal diseases can be in a number of categories: inflammatory, where tissue is destroyed by some process, for example Arthritis; degenerative, where the normal growth and renewal of tissues does not take place, as in Alzheimer's disease; or neoplastic, where there is abnormal growth in the tissues, as is the case with cancer. Diseases can also be caused by nutritional deficiencies, for example Beriberi, which results from a lack of vitamin B1 in the diet.

Unit 5, Lesson 5.2, Exercise D 🎧 1.22

Part 2

Actually, fighting disease is arguably the most important aspect of medicine. Regardless of how much you know about anatomy, physiology and their related chemical processes, a doctor who cannot diagnose disease in patients is not going to do them any good. So, it follows that it is important to have an excellent knowledge of the characteristics of diseases. What I mean is to know their causes and how they can be prevented or cured. So that's what the first stage is, getting to know what the various types of disease are.

But what are the various types of disease and how can we best identify them? Disease is found when variations occur in the normal structure or functions of the body, which give rise to problems or discomfort for the patient. There are many different ways of categorizing diseases. It can be by whether they can be passed on to others by those who have them, so that we get contagious, non-contagious, infectious and non-infectious diseases. We also get parasitic diseases such as malaria, where a parasite is responsible for the transmission.

Diseases can also be grouped in terms of their action on the body. There are three main types of action of this kind. Firstly, we have neoplastic diseases caused by abnormal growth. Secondly, there are degenerative diseases, caused by lack of growth. Finally, in this classification, there are inflammatory diseases where the cell's tissue is damaged. They can also be grouped by whether they are congenital diseases, which are from birth, or hereditary – passed on by parents. In addition, they can be classified in terms of the population groups they attack, such as maternal diseases, or in terms of the part of the body they attack, such as cardiac diseases.

So what can we do to lessen the effect that diseases have on our lives? Of course, we want to cure patients. But that is only one way in which we are useful in our role as doctors. In addition to curing people of diseases, another benefit we can provide is by preventing them from getting the disease in the first place. We have seen already what a powerful tool vaccination is and how it can prevent the spread of very dangerous diseases. A good example of this is the eradication of smallpox, which you came across earlier.

Unit 5, Lesson 5.2, Exercise E 🎧 1.23

Part 3

Anyway, er … to return to the main point – it's essential to identify population groups because the same type of intervention or treatment for a disease can be used with others in that group. Fundamentally, disease control is about having accurate data on disease levels within specific population groups. So how do we find out what these are? Well, one way to identify them is to look at the overall number of people in specific populations who have been diagnosed with a disease. This indicates the prevalence or extent of the disease in that population. We can then look at how many new cases of the disease are diagnosed in the population each year, which gives us the incidence of the disease. Sometimes, for practical reasons, we may need to estimate this based on a sample of the population. The number of people who die from the disease each year gives us the mortality rate. We can then analyze the prevalence, incidence and mortality rates of diseases as they are reported and look within these for population group characteristics. These can include age, gender (especially in the case of maternal diseases), income levels, geography, and whether individuals have an active or sedentary lifestyle – as in the case of coronary disease. Of these, geography, that is to say where people live, is probably one of the most important. Naturally, rates of prevalence, incidence and mortality between countries in the developed and developing world can be very different. For example, over 70% of mortality from AIDS in 2005 was in countries in sub-Saharan Africa (2 million out of 2.8 million worldwide). And the same variations are true of other diseases, particularly mortality from perinatal diseases, by which I mean those affecting children under one month old. By the way, AIDS and perinatal diseases are classified by the World Health Organization as communicable diseases, along with TB, malaria and other diseases which can be transmitted in some way. Non-communicable diseases refer to those which cannot be transmitted such as coronary disease. … Er … Where was I? Oh, yes …

Unit 5, Lesson 5.3, Exercise B 🎧 1.24

Part 4

So how it is possible to make predictions about what the incidence of disease on a global scale will be five, ten and twenty years from now? By research, obviously. There are several ways to categorize the types of research tools that are used. Let me see … one way is to distinguish between primary and secondary research. Another important distinction is between qualitative and quantitative research. However … oh, dear … sadly, I see that we've run out of time. This means that I'll have to ask you to do some research. I'd like you to find out what is meant by the four types of research I've just mentioned, that is, primary and secondary research, and qualitative and quantitative research. We'll discuss what you've found out next time I see you.

Unit 5, Lesson 5.3, Exercise C 🎧 1.25

1 'seminar

2 'overview

3 a'ssignment

4 'strategy

5 character'istics

6 suc'cessful

7 an'ticipate

8 'analyze

9 in'credibly

10 i'dentify

11 'category

12 va'riety

Unit 5, Lesson 5.3, Exercise D 🎧 1.26

Actually, fighting disease is arguably the most important aspect of medicine.

So, it follows that it is important to have an

excellent knowledge of the characteristics of diseases. What I mean is their causes and how they can be prevented or cured.

Anyway, er … to return to the main point – it's essential to identify population groups.

Fundamentally, disease control is about having accurate data on disease levels.

Naturally, rates of prevalence, incidence and mortality between countries in the developed and developing world can be very different.

Unit 5, Lesson 5.4, Exercise B 🎧 1.27

Extract 1

LECTURER: Right, Tomas and Leila, what did you find out about the world distribution of disease?

LEILA: Well, first of all, we looked in the University library to see whether they had any books or journals on the topic.

TOMAS: I don't like libraries.

Extract 2

LECTURER: And what else did you do?

LEILA: We talked to one of the librarians. She was quite helpful.

TOMAS: That's rubbish. She was really bored and didn't even look at us.

Extract 3

LECTURER: Leila, can you give us an explanation of your chart?

LEILA: Well, yes, it is a comparison between two countries; developed versus developing countries, and the rates of death from disease. And as you can see, we've put some different disease types on it.

LECTURER: What do the rest of you make of this? Evie, what about you?

EVIE: Well, erm … I'm not sure really.

Extract 4

LECTURER: Tomas, can you explain how you decided which disease types to put on your chart?

TOMAS: Well, yes, it's based on what we found in the report …

JACK: So it's primary.

Extract 5

LECTURER: What do you mean by 'primary', Jack?

JACK: I mean it's an example of primary research. They did two things – they looked for information in a report …

EVIE: Actually, that's secondary.

Unit 5, Lesson 5.4, Exercise C 🎧 1.28

Extract 6

LECTURER: Let's go back to this diagram for the moment to see how it can help with population grouping. First of all, tell us about the groupings you chose.

LEILA: Well, the report used death rates by country as the main way to distinguish the effects of the diseases. Didn't it, Tomas?

TOMAS: Absolutely. Those were really the only criteria they used. So that's why we chose them.

Extract 7

TOMAS: We used a list from one of the reference books the librarian showed us to decide on the disease types.

JACK: Sorry, I don't follow. Could you possibly explain why that's important?

TOMAS: Well, the figures were listed by actual disease – such as malaria – so we had to identify which disease types they belonged to in order to put them on the chart.

Extract 8

EVIE: I don't understand how you could decide which disease belongs to which disease type. We've already seen that diseases could fit into more than one category.

LEILA: Well, the librarian said that we should use our own judgement. For example, when we had to decide on infections in women who had just given birth we decided on maternal as the category, rather than infectious.

Extract 9

TOMAS: Yes, we wanted to put the diseases in the place they were most useful.

JACK: If I understand you correctly, you're saying

that even though they could be in more than one place, for the purposes of the chart you had to allocate them to the most likely type.

TOMAS: Yes, that's right.

Extract 10

LECTURER: This is all very interesting, isn't it?

EVIE: Yes, but if we just go back to the chart, the statistics show a huge difference in mortality rates from communicable diseases.

LEILA: Correct!

Unit 7, Lesson 7.2, Exercise B 🎧 2.1

Part 1

Good morning, everyone. What I'm going to talk about today is the medical treatment and care provided through our hospitals. Bearing in mind that hospital care comes in various different forms. The area of care that we are specifically going to focus on today is emergency care, which is also known as acute care. What I mean is the treatment of a disease or symptoms that require immediate attention; the care generally received by patients in Accident & Emergency. We'll also look at a typical patient journey. I'll go into more detail on this later. As for other aspects of patient care – primary care for example, we'll look at those later on, I mean, another time.

So, er … in later lectures, we'll also go on to consider how care is provided in different circumstances, such as primary or palliative care. Today, we will simply deal with the provision of acute or emergency care and the problems facing acute care hospitals today.

Unit 7, Lesson 7.2, Exercise C 🎧 2.2

Part 2

As you may already know, just over half of those entering a UK hospital on any given day are admitted in emergency circumstances as opposed to by appointment (in other words treatment that has been planned in advance). The emergency department encompasses all fields of medicine and surgery, and is responsible for patient admission, initial diagnosis and treatment. Medical practitioners working in emergency medicine possess a broad field of knowledge and procedural skills, including trauma resuscitation and surgical procedures, as well as advanced cardiac life support, etc. In other words, the average emergency doctor requires the skills of several different specialists at once; whether it be plastic surgery, to stitch complex lacerations, orthopaedics, for setting fractures, or simply ear nose and throat to stop a nose bleed. Not to mention gynaecology and cardiology. Indeed, he or she is required to deal with patients of all age groups and with the full spectrum of physical and behavioural disorders.

Unit 7, Lesson 7.2, Exercise E 🎧 2.3

Part 3

Now, an important concept in the smooth running of any hospital and one which frequently raises concern in the popular press is the notion of Integrated Care Pathway or ICP. So, what do I mean by the Integrated Care Pathway exactly? Well, to help you understand this concept, can you look for a moment at the patient leaflet that I have just handed out? As you can see, a patient typically arrives in admissions and then passes though several departments meeting different members of the emergency team before being discharged at the end of his or her stay. Let's look at an example of this. Say a patient arrives with a suspected fractured hip. After being admitted, the patient may spend time in the waiting room before being seen by the triage nurse who will assess their symptoms and vital signs. They will be then be sent for an X-ray before going to the Surgical Assessment Unit. Just prior to the operation the anaesthetist will make an assessment of the patient's fitness for operation. Immediately after the operation the patient will spend time in the recovery room, then go back to the orthopaedic ward. And then, finally the patient is discharged back to the care of their GP or family doctor. Despite significant advances in technology and increased specialization, the organization of these departments has changed very little. However, looking at it another way, changes in the patient mix and profile, an ageing population in effect, has brought about certain problems, notably an increase in admissions to acute care hospitals. And that's for both planned and emergency care. The point is that the resulting flow of patients is often inefficient and poorly coordinated. This is a phenomenon that has been noted in small regional hospitals as well as the

larger teaching hospitals. In financial terms, hospital wards are under pressure to close and the number of beds to be reduced. But why is 'patient flow' so important? Well, with hospitals that are capable of functioning to their optimal capacity, patient waiting times are reduced, the quality of care is improved and hospitals become more cost-effective; in this way maximizing the benefits of hospital care for all those who need it.

Unit 7, Lesson 7.2, Exercise F 🎧 2.4

Part 4

Now ... er ... let's see ... oh dear, I see we're running short of time ... but as we are discussing the patient journey perhaps I should just say something about the care cycle itself. Of course the care cycle is directly linked to the treatment a patient receives in hospital which in turn is linked to the idea of the Integrated Care Pathway that we talked about earlier.

The US Department of Health and Human Services has compiled a useful definition of a care cycle that can be applied to most diseases. At the centre of the cycle we have our patient and their condition; in other words, their disease, injury or disability. Then we have the five main stages of the care cycle. The problem with any cycle is where to start, so, for sake of argument, let's say that promotions and prevention is our first stage. What's different about the promotions and prevention stage is that it can be carried out on two levels simultaneously. On a general level, by targeting groups that are at risk of developing say ... heart disease. This is done by raising patient awareness through leaflets, anti-smoking campaigns, etc. And secondly, individually by encouraging screening: a good example of this is screening for breast or prostate cancers.

Once the complaint has been diagnosed we move on to stage two, the diagnosis stage. Following investigation, by carrying out a history, physical exam and lab work, the patient is diagnosed with a particular complaint. The treatment stage, which follows, might consist of surgery, a course of medication, or a plaster cast, for example, depending on the patient's condition. Stage four of our generic cycle is the management stage. In this stage of the cycle, stabilizing the patient and continuing with the prescribed treatment is of utmost importance. And this continues up to the moment the patient is discharged.

Lastly, there is rehabilitation. What's important about this stage is that by the end of it, the patient is once again able to function in his or her normal environment. Rehabilitation through physical and occupational therapy will start while the patient is still in hospital and then continue after he or she has been discharged.

Now ... oh dear, I was going to illustrate some specific examples of the care cycle, but ... ah ... I see that time is moving on. So instead, I'm going to ...

Unit 7, Lesson 7.3, Exercise A 🎧 2.5

1 a'cute

2 'discharge

3 i'nitiated

4 be'havioural

5 rehabili'tation

6 a'ccredited

7 pro'motion

8 simul'taneously

9 diag'nosis

10 pre'vention

11 ad'mission

12 e'mergency

Unit 7, Lesson 7.3, Exercise B 🎧 2.6

Part 5

I'm going to finish with some comments on medical training. Let's take training in the field of emergency medicine to continue with our general theme of the day. Now, the fact of the matter is, emergency medicine as a speciality is relatively young, something I'm sure you'll find rather surprising. ... Sorry ...

OK. Where was I? Oh, yes ... So when did emergency medicine (or EM) first come about? You've probably heard of the American physician, Dr James DeWitt Mills? It was Dr DeWitt Mills who established a system of 24-hour care at the Alexandria Hospital in Virginia in the 1960s. It

became known as the 'Alexandria Plan'. Prior to this, there were numerous problems with emergency care in US hospitals. Firstly, emergency care had been provided by any number of specialists – dermatologists, psychiatrists, etc., who would work on a rotation basis throughout the night. Not to mention the fact that interns, in other words physicians who were still in training, and even nurses, would also be drafted in to make up these emergency care teams. Plus, there's the fact that, in effect, these rather poorly organized emergency rooms, as they were known, were being run by medical staff, none of whom had been specifically trained in the field of emergency medicine. So, the result of the 'Alexandria Plan' was that the US media and various health reports published at the time were able to highlight the poor state of training in this particular field. Cincinnati General Hospital saw the first emergency medicine doctor in 1970 and it was in 1979 that the American Board of Medical Specialities finally recognized EM as a medical speciality.

Unfortunately, due to more recent changes, the level of effective acute care provision in our hospitals is now under threat. Let me put it another way ... hospitals now need to find alternatives to ease the strain and ultimately resolve the problem of overcrowded emergency departments.

Oh, I almost forgot to mention your research topics. OK, well, what's really important for the future of many national healthcare systems today is improving acute care provision. So I'd like you to find out what are the most appropriate means of reorganizing the emergency department. You may also want to consider what's currently being done in hospitals outside the UK.

Unit 7, Lesson 7.4, Exercise B 🎧 2.7

Extract 1

Now, as we know, the acute care hospital of the future will be vastly different from what we have come to know – the more ambulant or mobile patients and those that are considered 'less sick' will be managed elsewhere. I asked you to take a look at new ways of dealing with acute care provision in our hospitals. What did you discover? Do you agree that it is possible to reorganize the emergency care system? Don't forget you didn't have to limit your research to the UK. So, let's have some views.

Unit 7, Lesson 7.4, Exercises C and D 🎧 2.8

Extract 2

JACK: Well, I'd like to make two points. First, there are a great many patients that don't even need to visit A&E.

LEILA: Can you expand on that, Jack?

JACK: Well yes, these are what are known as the 'walking wounded', patients that have minor injuries or suspected fractures for example.

LEILA: So?

JACK: So the point is that these patients can probably be treated elsewhere, i.e., not in A&E.

LECTURER: OK. And what's your second point, Jack?

JACK: I was coming to that! My second point is that by taking these patients out of the equation we then free up medical staff in A&E to concentrate on more critical cases.

LEILA: Yes, but isn't the patient invariably going to be better off in a hospital environment?

MAJED: Well, I don't agree with that, Leila, because a noisy, overcrowded hospital isn't necessarily the best place for the patient to be anyway.

EVIE: Sorry, but what are we talking about, exactly? The care of the patients or how to improve 'patient flow'?

LEILA: Well, we need to be clear here. It has to be both, of course. Anyway, I'd just like to say that according to what I've read, nurses are now being trained to carry out duties that would once have been handled by doctors. As far as I see it the role of the nurse is a major factor in the reorganization of the Emergency Department.

EVIE: In what way?

LEILA: Well, these nurses are being trained to administer certain pain-relief drugs for example, as well as to do things like plaster casting, which is all very time consuming for the doctor.

EVIE: I don't get that. Why should nurses be doing the jobs that should be done by a doctor?

LEILA: It's not that they're doing the work of a doctor, as such. What I'm trying to say is, with nurses taking care of many of the minor conditions, emergency doctors are then able to spend time with the more serious cases. Nurses are simply being given a more important role.

MAJED: I still don't understand. Can you give me an example, Leila?

LEILA: OK. Look at it this way, as patients come into the Emergency Department, who is it they see first? The triage nurse – we saw this on the patient journey. If these nurses can assess the patient and then initiate minor treatment themselves, then the patient spends less time going from one department to another.

MAJED: So … the 'patient flow' is improved and waiting times are reduced. Plus we've improved the overall level of patient care and successfully reorganized the Emergency Department!

LEILA: Absolutely.

JACK: Interesting. I'd just like to suggest something else. If you think about it, we could extend that idea even further. I saw a documentary recently about a separate paediatric triage system that was being tested out in an Australian hospital. It showed children being assessed within a few minutes of arriving in Emergency. It's a more child-friendly environment and …

Unit 9, Lesson 9.2, Exercise B 🎧 2.9

Part 1

Good morning, everyone. I'm going to talk to you this morning about public health, and in particular, two very different public health issues that are affecting the health of the world today. I'm going to talk first about the topic of obesity and I will outline some of the major issues related to this current phenomenon. Then I will go on and do the same for climate change and its impact on health. I'll also give you a summary of the points we have covered.

But before we begin I have a little story to tell you. Before becoming a lecturer, I worked for Médicins du Monde. For those of you that haven't heard of it, it's an international humanitarian organization that provides medical care both in France and in the developing world. I was based in Haiti and it was a fantastic experience, at least from a personal point of view. I was working with children and young mothers and the team was just great. But as you can imagine the conditions were far from ideal: medical supplies were low and the conditions were just appalling. Consequently, there was a lot of frustration amongst the medical staff, as well as for the Haitians themselves. One of the biggest problems was corruption, the dishonesty of some of those in powerful jobs. Of course, the fact there wasn't any real public health system in place didn't help. It meant that supplies often didn't get through or they were hijacked on the way. And the ones that actually suffered the most were the kids ... Of course the point of that story was to illustrate the fact that the role of public health authorities in ensuring the health of a nation is crucial. So ... to get back to the main part of my lecture.

Now to start with, it might be useful to look at a definition of public health. Simply put, it's about improving the health of the community as a whole, as opposed to treating the individual. The United Nations World Health Organization (WHO) defines public health as 'a state of complete physical, mental and social well-being and not merely the absence of disease or infirmity'. As we shall see, the focus of public health is to prevent rather than treat disease and this is done by surveying cases and promoting healthy behaviour – on local and national levels as well as on an international level. It's worth pointing out here that a key point in public health is eliminating the disparities in health care – health care is, after all, one of the fundamental basic human rights along with access to clean drinking water and education. In terms of access to health care, unfortunately there are disparities not only between peoples of different ethnic origin but also gender. Gender gaps related to access to and control over resources are widespread. Possible exposure to health risks is fundamentally different between men and women.

What I'm going to focus on now is one particular subject for concern that is greatly affecting Western nations today and that, in many countries, has become an issue of public health.

OK, so to start with let's take a few moments to consider what constitutes obesity. What is it exactly that differentiates someone who is simply a little overweight with someone who we would classify as obese? When measuring weight, we usually use the body mass index, known as the BMI. To calculate someone's BMI, you take their weight in kilos and divide it by the square of their height in metres. Someone who is overweight would have a BMI equal to or more than 25 while someone who is 'obese' would have a BMI of 30 or more. Although, having said that, it could be argued that the risk of chronic disease as a result of obesity does in fact increase progressively from a BMI of 21. Anyway these are cut off points that provide a benchmark by which to assess individuals – adults of all ages and of both sexes. However, it should only be taken as a rough guide and it is not yet usable for children. The WHO is still in the process of developing a similar tool to measure childhood obesity. So, moving on, there are three important aspects to consider in terms of public health and obesity.

The first point is related of the extent of the problem. Research has shown that in 2005 approximately 1.6 billion adults – that's anyone aged 15 and above – were considered overweight and 400 million were classed as obese. One really alarming statistic is the 22 million children under the age of 5 that were overweight in 2007. Looking to the future, the WHO projections for people classed as overweight for 2015 are set at a staggering 2.3 billion worldwide with more than 700 million of those classed as obese.

Obesity was once considered a problem of high-income countries – the USA being the most obvious example. Increasingly, we find that now low- and middle-income countries are also falling victim to this epidemic. Malnutrition and obesity are just as likely to be found side by side within the same country. Indeed statistics show that more than 75% of overweight and obese children can be found in low- and middle-income countries.

So what causes obesity? Medically speaking the fundamental cause is an energy imbalance between calories consumed on the one hand and calories expended on the other hand. On a global level there has been a shift in diet towards the intake of what we consider energy-dense foods – in other words foodstuffs that are high in fat and sugar and low in vitamins, minerals and other micronutrients. Equally, intake of nutritional foodstuffs is falling. Coupled with this is the trend away from physical activity and the increasingly sedentary nature of our work. We can add to that greater reliance on modes of transport – as opposed to walking or cycling – and urbanization, i.e., the move away from the countryside into towns and cities.

Another major point is the related health risks that obese people run; in other words the consequences of obesity. It's probably fair to say that obesity as well as its related chronic diseases are largely preventable. And the risks people run are fairly well known. Common consequences of obesity include cardiovascular disease (strokes, heart attacks) which is the world's premier cause of death; over 7 million die of coronary heart disease worldwide. Also Type II diabetes – the WHO predicts diabetes-related deaths will rise by more than 50% in the next ten years. Other possible risks are osteoarthritis as a result of carrying excess weight. Other musculoskeletal disorders are also common, as are certain types of cancer – cancer of the colon, even breast cancer. People suffering from obesity also run the risk of suffering from respiratory problems and sleep apnoea. When it comes to clinically obese children, premature death and disability in adulthood are the long-term risks.

And now we come to the real question, which is what exactly are nations doing to reduce levels of obesity in their particular country? It's true to say that this epidemic extends beyond the medical sphere or even the educational sphere. We must accept that changes in policies in areas such as agriculture, food processing, marketing and distribution also play a significant role. From the point of view of the food industry as a whole, its contribution towards the eradication of obesity in children is crucial. Reducing the marketing of non-nutritious foods to children would be a huge step forward. Children under the age of eight are generally unable to understand the persuasive intent of advertising, and are not capable of viewing it critically. Instead they take it at face value. Research by the Institute of Medicine in the USA has shown that such marketing shapes their eating habits – habits that then last a lifetime.

So it should be clear that while public health authorities do have a role to play in attempting to eradicate this world phenomenon, regulating strategies aimed at improving consumer information and environmental influences also need to be understood and implemented appropriately. In an article by Mello et al, the authors decry the means employed by the US to date in this area. Crucially, they cite the results of previous public health victories, for example a reduction in the number of smokers, increased vaccinations and motor vehicle safety. These so-called victories had all been as a result of tighter public health legislation. I think this is a very interesting topic and definitely one that we can explore more later on. But now I want to turn now to climate change and the impact it is having on our health …

Unit 9, Lesson 9.2, Exercise C 🎧 2.10

Part 2

Let's turn now to the topic of global warming. We'll look at how it impacts on health first of all and then we'll consider the role of public health authorities and how they are dealing with the situation. I would be very surprised if anyone in this room had not heard of global warming. But have you ever stopped to think about the effects it may have on the health of the nation, indeed the planet? Before we go into the details in terms of health, I just want to look at the term 'global warming'.

You don't need to take notes on this, but I just want to give you a bit of background. According to the 4th Assessment Report of the IPCC, that's the Intergovernmental Panel on Climate Change, changes in lifestyle over the last 50 years have had an extremely negative effect on the atmosphere. In simple terms, roughly 66% of solar energy reaching the earth is absorbed by and heats the earth's surface. The heat then radiates back to the atmosphere where some of it is trapped by greenhouse gases, such as carbon dioxide. Over the last 50 years the burning of fossil fuels, for example, has released large quantities of CO_2 which have in turn had an affect on the climate.

Now where was I? Oh yes, right, I was talking about the effects of climate change on health. Of course, extremes of climate and weather can have both direct and indirect impacts on human life. Floods in Caracas in Venezuela in 1999 killed some 30,000 people. And Europe hasn't escaped such large-scale human loss either – the heatwave of 2003, for example, was linked to 35,000 deaths, mainly of the elderly, through heat stroke and dehydration.

Indirectly, there are differing effects of climate change depending on the source. Heatwaves, for example, mean increased UV exposure, which the UK Department of Health predicts will result in an extra 5,000 cases of skin cancer and 2,000 cases of cataracts per year by 2050. Higher temperatures also raise the possibilities of food poisoning, with an estimated 10,000 extra cases of salmonella infection per year in the UK. Higher temperatures also exacerbate the production of air pollutants. Air pollution in turn increases the frequency of cardio-vascular diseases and respiratory disorders, such as emphysema, asthma and allergies. Vector-borne disease – that's diseases transmitted by mosquitoes and ticks – would also be on the increase due to higher temperatures. In fact there is even a chance that malaria could be reintroduced into the UK. Storms, tornadoes and flooding not only give rise to injury from flying debris but also intestinal illnesses and other water-borne diseases brought about by the subsequent flooding of sewage treatment plants, as well as the possible exposure to hazardous toxic chemicals from runoff from agricultural land and urban storm-water systems. The Department of Health in the UK reports that flooding also leads to psychological problems; displaced persons can experience mental health consequences due to the stress of the immediate disruption to their lives not to mention enforced migration, be it only on a temporary basis. Crowded conditions in temporary shelters only further increase the risk of the spread of infectious disease.

So what exactly have we looked at this morning? Well, to sum up, we've looked at a definition of public health. I then went on to outline two major issues that are currently preoccupying public health authorities across the world – obesity and the impact of climate change on health. With obesity, we talked about the extent of the problem as well as its cause, the health risks of obesity and finally the measures being taken to resolve the problem. Secondly, with climate change, we looked at the direct followed by the indirect problems in terms of health brought about by climate change. Next, I want us to consider the role of public health authorities in preventing further negative effects from climate change …

Unit 9, Lesson 9.2, Exercise D 🎧 2.11

1   As we shall see, the focus of public health is to prevent rather than treat disease.

2   In terms of access to healthcare, unfortunately there are disparities not only between peoples of different ethnic origin but also gender.

3   It could be argued that the risk of chronic disease as a result of obesity does in fact increase progressively from a BMI of 21.

4   Research has shown that in 2005 approximately 1.6 billion adults – that's anyone aged 15 and above – were considered overweight and 400 million were classed as obese.

5   Increasingly, we find that now low- and middle-income countries are also falling victim to this epidemic.

6   It's true to say that this epidemic extends beyond the medical sphere or even the educational sphere.

7   From the point of view of the food industry as a whole, its contribution towards the eradication of obesity in children is crucial.

8   So it should be clear that while public health authorities do have a role to play in attempting to eradicate this world phenomenon, …

Unit 9, Lesson 9.3, Exercise A 🎧 2.12

1   'calculate, 'calorie, 'medical, over'weight, 'vitamin

2   childhood o'besity, 'heat stroke, physical ac'tivity, vector-borne di'sease

3   'breast cancer, family 'planning, 'gender gap, 'health risks

4   'actually, 'generally, 'usually, funda'mentally, 'crucially

Unit 9, Lesson 9.3, Exercise C 🎧 2.13

Part 3

OK, so moving on to look at some of the ways public health authorities are dealing with issues related to the effects of climate change on health.

Let's begin then with looking at who is responsible. In effect, we all have a role to play in combating the negative effects of climate change on our health. Individuals and businesses can take their own steps in reducing the burning of fossil fuels for example. National and local governments can enforce policies as well as put money into the assessment of health risks, early warning systems and plans for handling extreme weather. Public health practitioners are undoubtedly key players in this scenario, however. They can be working on improving primary healthcare for the vulnerable, taking measures to monitor health, and introducing better disease surveillance and disaster preparedness and vaccination, not to mention improving public education.

So let's look in a bit more detail at what is being done in the UK, as an example. One initiative is the heatwave plan that was introduced in 2004. The 'heat-health watch' operates from 1st June to 15 September each year and highlights responsibilities for health and social services once a heatwave has been identified – in the UK that's a temperature of 30°C during the day. Primary care trusts are required to issue advice to occupants and staff of residential homes for the elderly and help identify individuals most at risk from extreme heat. Meanwhile, public health regional directors are required to work with utility companies to maintain water and power supplies in affected areas.

Surveillance and control of infectious diseases is another priority. In 2002, a strategy was published for tackling infectious diseases. One of the outcomes was the increase in funding to improve diagnosis, treatment, prevention and control of infectious disease – be they water-, vector- or food-borne diseases. Providing clear advice and information is also crucial. The public needed to be more aware of the risks of infectious diseases and health professionals needed to be educated in recognizing and treating rare diseases that may appear more frequently as a result of climate change.

By the way, I see that some of you are using the Cornell note-taking system. That's very good. Do you all know about this? No? Right, well, if you want to know more about it, I suggest you look at How to study in college by Walter Pauk, the 9th edition, published in 2007. It's very good, and it should be in the university library. I'm sure that you all know the importance of taking good notes – and this system is particularly useful.

So to get back to the main topic … in other areas campaigns to increase public awareness have been implemented in an attempt to influence people's behaviour. These include information on early flood warnings and campaigns such as 'UK Sun Smart' on the risks of UV exposure.

In terms of health infrastructure in the country, public health authorities need to ensure they are able to cope with the predicted increased frequency of extreme events. This can be done by upping the number of specialists required in these areas of healthcare. The UK government has recognized the need to improve healthcare provision for those at-risk groups such as the elderly, the very young and the sick.

On a global level, the idea of the developed world helping the developing world has also been discussed. The UK definitely has a role to play in minimizing health impacts in developing countries, by improving healthcare provision through the training of healthcare professionals and relieving poverty.

OK, so now we can see that consideration of health impacts is a fairly recent development in the climate change debate, but one thing is certain – there exists a global responsibility. In fact, as Dr Georges Benjamin, Executive Director of the American Public Health Association points out in Principles of Public Health Medicine (one of your core texts – the 3rd

edition was published in 2006); rich countries have a special responsibility towards the developing world. Not only does the developing world emit the least greenhouse gases, it also possesses the fewest resources with which to cope with public health problems. One definition of public health given by thefreedictionary.com on the web is: 'the science and art of preventing disease, prolonging life and promoting health through the organized efforts and informed choices of society, organization, public and private, communities and individuals.' I think we can take that one step further and consider it as a global issue. To quote Benjamin: 'there is … an issue of disproportionate vulnerability. But in the industrialized world, because we live in a globalized economy, an increase in disease anywhere in the world really puts everyone at risk.'

Now I think that's all I'm going to say for the moment on the role of public health authorities on climate change. Are there any questions so far? No? Good. Now when I see you in tutorials we'll look in more detail at the role of public health institutions. In the meantime, I'm going to set you a research task. Right, now listen carefully … your task is to find out about how the public health sector in your particular country is dealing with the effects of climate change on the nation's health. I'd like you to work in groups of four. Each group should find out about one of the effects listed on the slide and report back on your findings.

Unit 9, Lesson 9.3, Exercise D 🎧 2.14

Extract 1

In fact, as Dr Georges Benjamin, Executive Director of the American Public Health Association points out in *Principles of Public Health Medicine* (one of your core texts – the 3rd edition was published in 2006); rich countries have a special responsibility towards the developing world.

Extract 2

By the way, I see that some of you are using the Cornell note-taking system. That's very good. Do you all know about this? No? Right, well, if you want to know more about it, I suggest you look at *How to Study in College* by Walter Pauk, the 9th edition, published in 2007. It's very good, and it should be in the university library.

Extract 3

One definition of public health given by *thefreedictionary.com* on the web is: 'the science and art of preventing disease, prolonging life and promoting health through the organized efforts and informed choices of society, organization, public and private, communities and individuals.'

Extract 4

I think we can take that one step further and consider it as a global issue. To quote Benjamin: 'there is … an issue of disproportionate vulnerability. But in the industrialized world, because we live in a globalized economy, an increase in disease anywhere in the world really puts everyone at risk.'

Unit 9, Lesson 9.4, Exercise C 🎧 2.15

Extract 1

It seems clear to me that the industrial world has a definite responsibility towards the developing world in terms of combating the impact of climate change on health. Let's look at three basic areas where such countries can help: firstly, in providing invaluable training for health care professionals in the developing world, in particular in specializations such as vector- and water-borne diseases – malaria for example; secondly, in donating funds for public health education to raise awareness of the health risks during extreme weather events – leaflets and campaigns; and thirdly, pretty important this, …

Extract 2

Erm, I think it is important first to define public health. This is very important. We can see, er, how this is important. So let's look at the slide and … oh sorry, that's the wrong slide, just a minute … right, so here is a definition of public health … er you can see I think, this is quite clear … do you have any questions about this slide?

Extract 3

We could ask the question: what is the impact of climate change on the developing world? From the point of view of the population, the health factor is just one issue but one that is related to both the economic and social impacts of extreme weather events, for example. Extreme weather brought about by climate change can affect living conditions; reduce access to clean drinking water, which in turn can cause problems in terms of health. Here we can look at some examples of this …

Extract 4

Countries such as the US and the UK have a very important role to play in reducing the health impact of climate change in poorer countries. In fact we could say that their input, both medically and financially, is crucial if the developing world is to survive extreme weather events in the future. If we look at the chart I've prepared here we can see the main countries affected by such events, and provision from richer countries. For example, if we examine in a bit more detail countries in the Africa region, we can see exactly where foreign resources to date have provided vital medical treatment …

Unit 11, Lesson 11.1, Exercise D 🎧 2.16

According to Beauchamp and Childers (2001), an ethical approach to medicine requires doctors to respect the principles of autonomy, beneficence, non-malfeasance and justice. These are implicit in most clinical guidelines, but there is a strong case for making them explicit.

Firstly, it could help in decision-making in the clinical setting. For example, a patient who is a Seventh Day Adventist may refuse to consent to treatment, such as a life-saving blood transfusion, on religious grounds. This is difficult for a medical practitioner because respecting the principle of autonomy means giving a person undergoing treatment the right to make decisions about their care. However, respecting the principle of beneficence obliges them to cure the sick person if possible. As a result of these conflicting requirements, physicians can face an ethical dilemma. If local clinical guidelines explicitly state the ethical principles, doctors can be sure their decisions are ethically sound. Moreover, the caregiver can clearly explain the ethical grounds for decisions, which helps the doctor to preserve the patient's dignity.

Secondly, if the principle of justice is applied in the guidelines, doctors find it easier to justify their choice of treatment to patients. For example, national guidelines on recommended drugs are not always applied uniformly. One result is that patients may not get the most effective one for their condition and so are likely to complain. If the ethical reasons for the choice are made clear, the doctor can explain these to the patient. Finally, by clarifying the underlying ethical principles, those called upon to apply them can see inconsistencies much more easily.

Unit 11, Lesson 11.2, Exercise B 🎧 2.17

Part 1

Good morning. My name is Dr Balbir Singh and much of my work has been in areas related to medical ethics. I'm here today to give you an overview of ethical and legal issues you are likely to encounter when dealing with patients, that is to say I am going to look at the ethico-legal issues relating to patients.

Don't misunderstand me, I don't want you to assume that medical ethics are relevant only when dealing directly with patients. As we all know, to some degree, ethical considerations will form a part of every decision you make as a doctor, regardless of your role. However, it's fair to say that legal and ethical issues are most apparent when dealing directly with patients. Not only that, but they become more emotional as well. We can think of many such cases – for example, patients who want to end their lives because of their condition, women past child-bearing age who want to have children, patients who demand non-standard treatments, and when to stop life support for an elderly patient. As you can see, the range is very wide indeed. So in an attempt to keep the discussion on ethical issues reasonably simple, I'm going to summarize the background to some of the key issues around consent in patient treatment and clinical research.

Unit 11, Lesson 11.2, Exercise C 🎧 2.18

Part 2

To start with, it is important to understand the background to the current ethico-legal framework in which doctors have to operate. To some degree what we understand by medical ethics goes back as far as the 4th century and the establishment of the Hippocratic Oath. It is often assumed that the principles underpinning this have simply been refined and developed over time by the legal and medical professions to give us our current ethico-legal framework. Actually, and this may surprise many of you, the starting point for current ethical standards only dates back to 1945, when the Nuremberg Code was drawn up. At the end of the Second World War, it became clear that that, during the war, many medical experiments in

Germany caused great suffering, to the extent that thousands of prisoners died or were disfigured. A case in point is the experiments in which prisoners were immersed in ice-cold water to measure how long they could survive.

It was primarily to clarify what was acceptable in the conduct of experiments on humans that the Nuremberg Code was drawn up. At the centre of the code was the need for the voluntary consent of the human subject to any procedures they would undergo. Weindling (2005) gives a very good description of the process in his book *Nazi Medicine and the Nuremberg Trials*.

However, while it provided ethical guidance in the context of experimentation on human subjects, the Nuremberg Code did not concern itself with the relationship between the doctor and the patient outside the experimental situation. It was only with the issuing of the Declaration of Helsinki in 1964 by the World Medical Association that this point was addressed. The Declaration stated that not only must participation in any research be a voluntary choice, it must also be an informed one. A useful editorial from the BMJ on the subject explains how it came about and its importance. It is fair to say that the declaration has provided the basis for the development of the medico-legal ethics we apply today. This had important implications for all doctors, because for the first time it was recognized that there was a need to obtain informed consent from patients for professional care which included research.

So what about examples in practice of obtaining informed consent to treatment? Obtaining written consent to perform an operation is a routine task, undertaken on a daily basis. Some doctors may say that in practice its only real function is obtaining proof of consent for invasive actions, which could otherwise be legally considered assault. They feel that the patient does not have enough medical knowledge and expertise to evaluate the risks and benefits of a procedure, even when they have sufficient information to do so. In the opinion of this section of the medical profession, it is only the doctor who is in a position to make a fully informed, objective judgement. I simply cannot agree with this position, which can only be described as misguided paternalism. I mean, it's like the doctor behaving as a parent, not a professional advisor. Ensuring a patient is fully aware of the risks and benefits of a procedure is not only a legal requirement, in order to prevent accusations of medical negligence on your part, but it is also fundamental to the ethical principle of patient autonomy.

Some doctors may believe that by signing the consent form, the patient indicates that they have understood the information they have been given. The evidence shows that this may not be the case. A very useful article by Sudore et al. (2006) in the Journal of General Internal Medicine outlines an experiment carried out to measure how much of the information in consent forms was understood by patients. Briefly, she explains how in fact only 28% of patients presented with a highly simplified medical consent form fully understood it the first time. In my view this very strongly supports the need for greater care when gaining consent to procedures. In particular, it is necessary to provide the information in a way which the patient can understand, and to check that they have indeed understood what you have told them. With respect to Sudore's study, she points out that regardless of how highly literate anybody is, we cannot assume that they understand the medical consent information we provide them with. She has no doubt that this is one of the most important factors which legislators have to consider in relation to patient consent.

There are also a number of practical considerations to take into account when obtaining patient consent for treatment, which I am only going to touch on here. If you want to look more closely at these, a very good overview can be found in the Student BMJ (I'll give you the URL later). Perhaps the most important consideration is that the patient should be legally entitled to give their consent to the procedure. As a rule, all adults can give consent, except for those whose reason is impaired, for example by drink or drugs or as a result of mental illness. Minors in the US cannot give consent, while those in the UK, Canada or Australia can if they are judged mature enough, according to what is known as the 'Gillick standard'.

Now I'm going to pause at this point and ...

Unit 11, Lesson 11.2, Exercise F 🎧 2.19

Some doctors may believe that by signing the consent form the patient shows they have understood the information they have been given. The evidence shows that this is not the case. A very useful article by Sudore et al (2006) in the *Journal of General Internal Medicine* showed that in fact only 28% of patients presented with a highly simplified medical consent form fully understood it first time. In my view this very strongly supports the need for greater care when gaining consent to procedures. In particular, it is necessary to provide the information

in a form which the patient can understand, and to check that they have indeed understood what you have told them. As Sudore points out, regardless of how highly literate anybody is, we cannot assume that they understand the medical consent information we provide them with.

Unit 11, Lesson 11.2, Exercise G 🎧 2.20

Extract 1

I'm here today to give you an overview of ethical and legal issues you are likely to encounter when dealing with patients, that is to say I am going to look at the ethico-legal issues relating to patients.

Extract 2

Don't misunderstand me, I don't want you to assume that medical ethics are relevant only when dealing directly with patients.

Extract 3

As we all know, to some degree, ethical considerations will form a part of every decision you make as a doctor, regardless of your role.

Extract 4

However, it's fair to say that legal and ethical issues are most apparent when dealing directly with patients.

Extract 5

Not only that, but they become more emotional as well.

Extract 6

So in an attempt to keep the discussion on ethical issues reasonably simple, I'm going to summarize the background to some of the key issues around consent in patient treatment and clinical research.

Extract 7

... it became clear that during the war, many medical experiments in Germany caused great suffering, to the extent that thousands of prisoners died or were disfigured.

Extract 8

A case in point is the experiments in which prisoners were immersed in ice-cold water to measure how long they could survive.

Extract 9

Weindling (2005) gives a very good description of the process in his book *Nazi Medicine and the Nuremberg Trials*.

Extract 10

With respect to Sudore's study, she points out that regardless of how highly literate anybody is, we cannot assume they understand the medical consent information we provide them with.

Extract 11

Briefly, she explains how in fact only 28% of patients presented with a highly simplified medical consent form fully understood it the first time.

Extract 12

She has no doubt that this is one of the most important factors which legislators have to consider in relation to patient consent.

Unit 11, Lesson 11.3, Exercise A 🎧 2.21

biomedical re'search

informed con'sent

'research subject

legal regu'lation

moral 'rights

the degree of 'risk

research 'protocols

research 'governance

Unit 11, Lesson 11.3, Exercise B 🎧 2.22

Part 3

Turning now to the ethical and legal issues relating to biomedical research, the question is in what way do these differ from those relating to treatment? As with decisions on treatment, while the ethical principles we discussed earlier are key, the legal aspects are equally important. In the UK for example, local Research Ethics Committees (RECs) are responsible for research governance. Their job is to check research protocols – the guidelines that set out how the study is to be undertaken, and to make sure that they meet the necessary ethical standards. As part of this, they will evaluate the risks and benefits from a medical perspective, deciding whether the research is worthwhile or too risky.

Ethics committees will also want to ensure that when the participants have consented, it is informed consent. It is quite clear that the research subjects must be given accurate and detailed information on the risks they face, so they can evaluate them for themselves and refuse to participate, if they wish. Informed consent also requires that they are given information about the goals, methods and possible benefits of the research. The confidentiality of the information gathered in the course of the research is also of key importance. In general, ethics committees will want to see details of how data is to be collected, stored and used in order to ensure the privacy of participants is not compromised. In most developed countries these requirements all have the force of law. For example in the UK, since 2007, drug trials cannot be conducted without the agreement of an REC.

It is clear therefore that compliance is not simply a matter of recognizing participants' moral rights but of legal regulation. The question is then: is this legal regulation justified? There are those who claim that imposing this regulation on research simply increases the time needed to bring drugs onto the market, which may cost people their lives. I'm afraid that just isn't true. It's quite clear that without this protection, more people taking part in trials could suffer harm and even death. The research has concluded that regulatory regimes do much to protect patients from unsafe and ineffective drugs and help safeguard the health of the volunteers who test them. For example, in 2006 in the UK, the lives of six volunteers in a clinical trial were saved due to the strict protocols under which the trial was conducted. It is my opinion that for this reason the increased cost of regulation can be justified. However, this protection is not uniformly applied. There is evidence to suggest that, increasingly, drug companies are conducting their tests outside the developed world, for example in Africa and Asia, where research regulatory regimes are less strict.

Perhaps the best example of what can happen without a clearly defined system of regulation for biomedical research comes from the Tuskegee study of untreated syphilis in the Negro male, to give it its full title. Initiated in 1932, in the United States, it enrolled 399 participants to act as a control group against which various treatments for syphilis could be evaluated. However, by 1947 penicillin had emerged as an effective cure for syphilis, ending the need for the trial. Despite this, the researchers actively prevented the control group participants from getting treatment for their condition. By the time the research was halted in 1972 (due to adverse press coverage), 28 had died of syphilis and another 100 from related conditions. Not only had the researchers failed to obtain informed consent from the participants, they had put the goal of completing the study before that of the participants' welfare, which is clearly against the principle of non-malfeasance. It is not surprising that Katz et al. (2006) referred to it as 'arguably the most infamous biomedical research study in US history'. As a result of being famous for the wrong reasons, it has played a part in the ongoing debate between academics about the effect it has had on the numbers of minorities recruited to clinical trials.

Well, it looks as if I'm running out of time. Before I finish, I'm going to set you a task that will involve investigating some of the points I've raised. I want you to do some research to identify examples of situations where doctors' decisions regarding patients involve a conflict between two or more of the main ethical principles in medicine. The examples can relate to patients in either research or treatment situations. Try to look into specific cases to substantiate your arguments. If possible, I'd like you to think about whether it is possible to resolve the conflicting principles in the examples identified.

Unit 11, Lesson 11.3, Exercise E 🎧 2.23

It is clear therefore that compliance is not simply a matter of recognizing participants' moral rights but of legal regulation. The question is then: is this legal regulation justified? There are those who claim that imposing this regulation on research simply increases the time needed to bring drugs onto the market, which may cost people their lives. I'm afraid that just isn't true. It's quite clear that without this protection, more people taking part in trials could suffer harm and even death. The research has concluded that regulatory regimes do much to protect patients from unsafe and ineffective drugs and help safeguard the health of the volunteers who test them. The evidence lies in the fact that in 2006 in the UK, the lives of six volunteers in a clinical trial were saved due to the strict protocols under which the trial was conducted.

Unit 11, Lesson 11.4, Exercise E 🎧 2.24

Extract 1

MAJED: I'd like to start by explaining why I would like to focus on legal cases relating to patient consent to treatment. As well as the issue of informed patient consent, which is relevant, we can also look at a very different issue – which is whether legal decisions are in line with medical ethics. Cases I have identified include one in which a patient had legs removed in order to save his life. The patient went to court because he felt that he would not have consented to have his legs removed under any circumstances. The doctor argued that the ethical (and legal) obligation was to save the patient's life before anything else. There is also a case of a doctor who removed a woman's womb in which he discovered a cancer while he was operating for something else. It sounds like fascinating stuff. Does anybody have any opinions or anything they would like to add?

Extract 2

EVIE: Thanks, Majed. I don't have anything to add, does anybody else? No. OK, following on from what Majed has said, I would like to look at how ethical dilemmas can arise in obtaining consent in relation to research, focusing on the conflict between the benefits and the risks to people participating in experiments. I've looked at the websites of companies who recruit volunteers for trials and one of the reasons they give is that taking part in trials helps provide drugs to tackle the diseases of the future. It is true that without trials there wouldn't be new drugs, but I don't think that is the main reason most people take part. Most of the websites focus on the money volunteers can make and how easy it is. In my opinion it is very difficult to have an ethical balance between paying people to take part and expecting them to give informed consent which is not influenced in any way. I'm going to expand the topic by looking at whether regulation in the UK and other countries means that more trials are taking place in countries in Asia and Africa.

Extract 3

JACK: That seems like a very good point Evie is making about the effect of regulation on drug trials. To carry on from this point, I want to look at what exactly these regulations require the companies running tests to do, comparing how they work in a number of different countries. This should allow me to compare the benefits of extensive testing and the difficulty it presents in terms of getting new drugs onto the market. I'm going to expand on the topic by looking at examples of drugs which have been tested extensively, have gone onto the market and then been withdrawn because they are unsafe. This could show whether or not the level of regulation is high enough to protect patients.

Extract 4

LEILA: Thank you, Jack. That sounds like a very interesting topic. As well as looking how to balance patient safety and the need for new drugs, we can also look at a very different issue. This is the issue of the extent to which we can use patient data to carry out research on specific conditions, without needing to gain the patient's consent every time we use the data. For example, at the moment, if data is gathered on a patient in the course of treatment, it cannot be used for research purposes unless the patient authorizes it. Gaining that authorization can be a long and time-consuming process. By carrying out research using this data, it could be possible to come up with new ways of treating the condition which would benefit not only the patient, but others as well. So to sum up, we can say that I will be looking at the balance of the patient's right to confidentiality against the wider public interest.